EARN MONEY TYPING AT HOME

A complete guide to
freelancing your typing and
word processing skills

BY

ROBERT HANCOCK

and

ELIZABETH ASHTON

BROUGHTON HALL, INC.
Revised Fourth Edition
Copyright © 1998

ISBN 0-934748-36-5

Manufactured in the United States of America

PUBLISHER'S NOTE

We have done our best to carefully research and compile this Directory only from sources believed to be authentic and reliable. However, we cannot guarantee total accuracy or completeness.

If you would be kind enough to bring to our attention any errors you may find, we will include your corrections in our next edition. We will also send you a complimentary bonus report as a token of our appreciation.

Please note we are publishers and are not affiliated in any way with any of the organizations or businesses listed in this Directory. Our sole purpose is to provide you with a fund of useful information.

The Publishers

TABLE OF CONTENTS

1.0 <u>INTRODUCTION</u>

Typing ability — or to use the modern phrase, "keyboarding skills" — can be a highly marketable commodity. If you are already a competent typist, or if you can polish rusty typing skills, you can do something that other people can't do, and something that they need to have done.

This, in case you haven't already realized it, is the simple formula for success in any business. Find out what the market needs; sell it at a fair price; and **you** are well on the way to being a successful independent businessman or businesswoman.

What is more, it is a business you can get into with very modest expenditure, at least initially — though as the volume of your business grows, you may be surprised at how easily and naturally you invest in new equipment and new technology (such as a fax machine) to improve your productivity and, of course, your income.

1.1 <u>IS IT FOR YOU?</u>

The phrase "independent businessman or businesswoman" may be a bit frightening: doesn't it mean a lot of responsibility and hard work? Well, yes and no. If you can take the responsibility and hard work of raising a family, running a business should not alarm you too much. And if, when you were at school, you could deliver assignments on time — isn't that very much like running your own typing business?

Within reason, typing at home is a business that **anyone** can get into. You've got to be able to read and write, of course, and you've got to be able to use a typewriter. After that, it is down to how much **you** are willing to put into it. No one will pay you for doing nothing, or for turning in sloppy work; but they will pay you, and pay you well, for good work that is delivered on time.

Why do it?

The great thing about typing at home is that it is *at home*. You can fit your hours around your other commitments, whether those commitments are to work, play or family. If you are naturally a "morning person," you can start work at dawn (or earlier); if you are a "night person," you can work far into the night.

You don't waste long hours commuting — and, of course, you don't face that icy blast as you step out of the door to go to work on a winter's morning. Your "commute" is entirely inside your own home, unless you decide that you would rather rent a small office somewhere nearby (perhaps near your main pool of clients) and work from there.

What You Earn, You Keep

Another major advantage is that neither you nor your customers are paying a middleman — a typing agency — who demands a slice of the action. This is an advantage that works two ways.

One is when you are working for a big company. Here, reliability and quality are more important than price, so you can charge as much (or very nearly as much) as the established agencies, and the money is all yours, at least after taxes. The **minimum** an agency charges today is likely to be close to $10 an hour, even in a small town, while agencies in the big city can charge twice as much, so you can see that the potential for money-making is considerable!

The other is that many people who wouldn't hire someone from a major agency — because of minimum-hours requirements, bureaucracy, form-filling and other hassles — may well be willing to hire *you*. They may not pay as well as the big companies, but there are many, many more of them.

1.2   WHO HIRES HOME TYPISTS?

Anyone who needs typing done, and can't get it done elsewhere, will hire home typists. A friend of mine used to work for a Hollywood television production company that was always sending out scripts to be typed. Apart from the glamour of being associated with Hollywood, even on the very edge of the business, the production company didn't care what they paid typists who worked for them (within reason, anyway): all they cared about was **fast, reliable** typing.

At the other extreme, many people hire typists even when they are carefully watching the pennies. Until I got my keyboard skills up to semi-professional levels, I used to hire typists all the time to do final copies of manuscripts, to type up proposals, to take care of my mail while I was travelling (I still do that), and to revise already-typed materials that I had covered with marginal notes and comments. I wasn't about to use expensive agencies and office service bureaus, where I was just another face: Patsy, with her trusty electric typewriter, was (and is) a friend as well as an indispensable business assistant.

Speed and Reliability

When you're working for yourself, "speed" doesn't mean quite the same as it does when you're in an office. Your clients don't care whether you type twenty words a minute, or a hundred and twenty. What they care about is that you meet deadlines. If you say you will have a completed script with them by the end of the month, or a letter by tomorrow, then that is what you have to do. One late delivery, and your reputation is suspect; two, and you've blown it.

Reliability means much the same thing, *plus* accuracy. As long as your work is "clean" (without errors, gallons of white-out, and other faults), you are delivering what people want.

Repeat Business

The ideal, for anyone running a business of this kind, is to have clients calling **you**. You know you've made it when they call you and ask, "Is there any chance that you could ..."

When that happens, it means that two things have happened. The first is that they are treating you as an equal, as a fellow human being, instead of a piece of office furniture to be used.

The second is that they realize they are not the only client: they are treating you as a fellow professional, someone whose work is as important as theirs, and without whom they cannot function. If you have previously worked in an old-fashioned office where you were the bottom of the heap, this alone can make it worthwhile to work for yourself!

Until you have established your reputation, though, you are going to have to go out and hustle for business. This is not much fun, and there are times when it is downright discouraging. In Chapter 4, though, you can get a lot of ideas about who to approach and how to approach them, and Chapter 7 gives you more ideas about where to look to find details of businesses in **your** community. The rest of this book is about how to deliver the kind of work that builds your reputation (and your income) to the kind of levels you want.

1.3   WHAT THIS BOOK CAN (AND CANNOT) DO

One thing I can't do in this book, unfortunately, is to provide you with a comprehensive listing of people who want typing done. The good news, though, is that I can't do this because there are simply too many people in the country who are potential customers! I couldn't even do it if the book were six inches thick: that might be enough for all the potential customers in a single state, provided it wasn't a very busy state! To provide a full listing would take shelf upon shelf of directories, and most of them would not be much use to you anyway: if you live in the Midwest, a listing of small businesses in New York City would not do you much good, and the same would be true for a listing of Iowa businesses if you lived in Chicago.

What I **can** do, though, is tell you what sort of local directories may be available in *your* area, and tell you the best way to use them. Chapter 7, RESOURCES, is about this, and about government and other agencies which exist to help *you*.

Before going on to the "nitty-gritty" of working for yourself, it is worth looking at how business works in the 1990's: if your view of office life is even a few years out of date, you may be amazed at how much things have changed!

1.4 THE OFFICE OF THE 90's

The traditional office, with its "bull pen" of young executives, its serried ranks of typists, its Vice Presidents on the next-to-top floor, and its President in lonely splendor in the penthouse, is as out-of-date as the quill pen and the stagecoach. Many such offices still survive, but they are dinosaurs; their day is past.

The modern office is more concerned with "go" than with "show." Oh yes, a modern company still needs *somewhere* as a headquarters, and those headquarters may well be very comfortable and luxurious; but with modern telecommunications and good management, the people who work for the company may be spread across a city, across a state, across the nation, or even around the world.

"On-Demand" Skills

There is also more call for "on-demand" skills. Instead of paying someone to sit in their office day after day, whether they are working or not, a modern company pays to have a job done. If they can "buy in" that job, so much the better for them: they pay people when they are working, and pay them well. If there's no work, they are not stuck with the expensive overhead of people, floor space, equipment, and all the other fixed costs that made the old-style corporate headquarters so prohibitively expensive.

Now, this may be bad news for employees – but for you, as an independent entrepreneur, it's great news. The Widget Corporation needs typing done? *Great:* they need you (or someone much like yourself) to do it. The Widget Corporation is having a bad time, with a hostile takeover bid, and won't give you any more work? *Who cares?* Shyster, Flywheel and Shyster are initiating the corporate takeover, and their secretaries can't handle all the work – so who do they turn to? You! The takeover is finished; the Widget Corporation has gone bankrupt; Shyster, Flywheel and Shyster have lost their biggest client and are laying off their own secretaries, never mind cutting all outside contracts? Well, never mind: the local Parks and Recreation Department needs its spring schedule typed …

1.5 THIS IS THE FUTURE

The thing is, the organizations who work by buying in the talent they need are often the best-managed and most competitive in their respective fields, so chances are that if you can build a small, reliable client list, you will have all the work you need, for as long as you need it. No one company is going to employ you full time — if they did, it really would be cheaper for them to have an on-site typist — but some people get by with client lists that consist of only half a dozen corporations and individuals, while others enjoy the challenge of working for dozens of different organizations, never knowing what is going to come "over the transom" tomorrow.

As a part of this revolution in business, *you* are very well placed: you are getting in on the ground floor. In ten year's time, it may well be that the majority of businesses work in the way that I have already described. By that time, you could be running your own typing bureau, assigning clients to typists and typists to clients ....

1.6   MAKING THE TRANSITION

At the moment, our market research at Broughton Hall shows that you are probably one of three kinds of people.

One kind is someone who is already employed, but who wants either to earn extra money by "moonlighting" or to escape the nine-to-five routine.

The second kind is someone who has typing skills, but who (usually for no fault of his or her own) is temporarily unemployed. This comes back to what I said a few paragraphs back — the office of the 1990's is bad news for employees, but good news for people who want to work independently.

The third kind is the mother (or more rarely, father) with young children, who cannot work outside the house or who prefers to be with her or his children rather than putting them in daycare and going out to work.

Begin by "Moonlighting"

Quite honestly, you would be rash to throw over an existing job and go straight into typing for a living, unless you have some savings to tide you over while you gain experience. It takes time to build a client list. Go into it part-time, or begin with a few hours a day for a few days a week. That way, you can find out how much work you can realistically do; how much work you **want** to do; and indeed, whether typing at home is what you really want to do at all. It's a great opportunity, but (like any other job) it's not necessarily what everyone wants to do.

Consider "Temping"

If you possibly can, you should consider working for a temporary agency for a while before you take the big step and become a full-time freelance. This shows you what businesses expect, and gives you an excellent insight into today's changing business life.

It also gives you experience in a wide range of different businesses, all of which can be extremely useful when you decide to go into business for yourself. If you have already worked for a small manufacturing company, a lawyer and a dentist, you will be much better placed to understand what those different types of businesses are looking for when they hire a home typist — and to make your "sales pitch" appropriately.

There are general things you can learn, too: one office might have a particularly good filing system, while another handles mailing lists unusually well. Keep your eyes open, and learn all that you can — don't just focus on your own immediate job. You can put all this experience to work when you go into business for yourself.

Don't Do Too Much, Too Soon

Obviously, you don't want to go in over your head, either financially or personally. On the other hand, the more you give, the more you get. Copy-typing an author's manuscript (Chapter 4) is easy enough, and might pay $5 to $10 per hour, or even more in a large city where there are more authors and fewer typists. On the other hand, it's a "on-off" sort of job: few authors are prolific enough to keep you in full-time business!

"Sorting out" a badly drafted report could easily earn twice or even three times as much per hour, though, and this **is** something which can lead to more and more work. And if you can offer secretarial services, like my friend Patsy, you should be able to build up a solid, reliable client list of people who will give you all the work you want.

Adding Other Strings to Your Bow

You may find it useful to check some other Broughton Hall titles, such as *Jobs at Home*, to see if there are other things you want to mix with your typing — for example, reading books for money. If you have two or three strings to your bow, you are going to be even better placed in tomorrow's competitive jobs marketplace.

Where to Work

Finding a place to work means striking a three-way balance between convenience, privacy, and expense. What you *can't* do, except for the very lightest amount of work, is to use the kitchen table or dining-room table. Sure, you may have enough space to set up a typewriter and spread out your papers; but you'll have to clear everything away each time you want to use the table for anything else. If you have a family, or even roommates, you may well find that you have to fight for your territory at times when you need to be left alone.

The ideal is to have a room set aside as an office and nothing else, but plenty of people work successfully at home without this. Many people use a spare bedroom as a guestroom-cum-office, and I know one very successful Hollywood casting agent whose "office" is actually a large closet lined with shelves and filing cabinets. You *must*, however, have somewhere that your typewriter or word processor can be left set up, and where you will not constantly be troubled by other people: this can be very important if you have children in the house! Of course, if you live alone, you can work anywhere you like. I know a freelance photographer who has also written several books, and his office *is* actually in his kitchen. In all fairness, it is a very large kitchen in a 150-year-old cottage, and his desk is a long way from the stove.

You also need to have all your supplies conveniently at hand, in a place where they will not be "borrowed" by everyone else in the house: paper, ribbons, stapler, paper clips and so forth.

At the very least, therefore, you need a corner of a room that is *yours* and is respected as such. Everyone must understand that it is off limits unless you give them special permission to be there — and that NO ONE *EVER* puts coffee cups down on the desk. This includes you! Coffee-cup rings can be a problem enough; a knocked-over cup of coffee can destroy a week's work and even (if you are really unlucky) short out electrical equipment.

"Home" and "Office"

Keeping coffee off your desk is not the only kind of self-discipline that you need. For a start, you need to be able to resist the siren call of the refrigerator and the cookie-jar, or you will not just fall behind with your work: you will get fat as well. You need to remember that time spent away from your desk is money not earned, and this is as true whether you are reading to your four-year-old or drinking coffee with a friend. You need, in fact, to be able to split your personality a little bit, so that you are "at home" and "out" at the same time. There is more about this in Chapter 2.

Because of these limitations, some "home-based" workers decide instead to rent an office, and to work from there. At first, this is almost certainly "overkill" for most people, so I'll leave it until Chapter 6, "Coping with Success."

Now, let's look at the starting point: What skills have you got to take to the market place?

2.0 SELLING YOUR SKILLS

Before you can sell your skills, you need to make a realistic assessment of what they are. The first and most important thing to realize is that *speed* comes second to *quality*. As long as you do the work properly, you will get repeat business; but if you turn in work that is marred with mistakes and covered with white-out fluid, no one is going to bother to use you again. In other words, you can start out slow because you can always get faster, but it won't do you any good at all to start out bad on the assumption that you can get better.

Even so, it is useful to know how fast you can reliably type. If you have not been tested for a while, a cheap way to find out your speed level is to go to a local temp agency. They almost always test typing speed (and shorthand speed, if you have shorthand) before they take you on. You may or may not want to work for them for awhile, though you should consider it as a means of gaining experience, and it's a good way to get tested.

2.1 ADDITIONAL SKILLS

I have already mentioned typing and shorthand, and this leads on to the next question: what other skills have you? These can be divided into two groups: secretarial skills and experience.

It may seem strange to refer to "experience" as a skill, but that is what it is! Suppose, for example, that you have worked as a legal secretary. This obviously makes you more attractive to a lawyer who needs some typing done.

Not only that, many skills are "transferrable." Suppose you have worked in a school, typing up academic records. Well, academic records are not much different from medical records or legal records. The technical terms are going to be different, and possibly more difficult, in the legal and medical fields — but hey, you're a professional typist! You can learn!

Using the checklist on the opposite page, make a list of *your* skills. Rate your skills and experience as follows:

1   No skill or experience

2   Slight experience; some skill

3   Average skill or experience

4   Better-than-average skill or experience

5   Expert

No one is likely to be an expert in all these fields, but there may be whole other areas where you know a great deal. Use the extra lines at the foot of the checklist to fill these in.

SKILL AND EXPERIENCE CHECKLIST

	1	2	3	4	5
Typing	—	—	—	—	—
Shorthand	—	—	—	—	—
Filing	—	—	—	—	—
Data Entry	—	—	—	—	—
Word Processing	—	—	—	—	—
Typing Numbers or Statistics	—	—	—	—	—
Typing Records	—	—	—	—	—
Medical	—	—	—	—	—
Legal	—	—	—	—	—
Wholesale	—	—	—	—	—
Retail	—	—	—	—	—
Academic	—	—	—	—	—
Large Businesses	—	—	—	—	—
Small Businesses	—	—	—	—	—
Liaison with other people	—	—	—	—	—
Working under pressure	—	—	—	—	—
_____	—	—	—	—	—
_____	—	—	—	—	—
_____	—	—	—	—	—
_____	—	—	—	—	—
_____	—	—	—	—	—

2.2   <u>TYPEWRITERS AND TYPING</u>

Although this book is called *Typing at Home*, I have to be honest: a typewriter is only just sufficient if you want to make a living in today's highly automated office environment. Only if you are an absolutely first-class typist can you provide the kind of error-free finish that comes automatically when you use a word processor.

If you have been out of the work place for a few years, or if you are still working in an office that has typewriters, you cannot imagine how much better a computer is than a typewriter. For example, I mistyped "typewriter" as "typtewriter" in the last sentence, and correcting it took only a moment on the word processor keyboard. Even if I had spotted it early, using a typewriter with a "lift-off" correction ribbon, it would still not have looked as good as the print from my printer.

What is more, you can save *all* your clients' work electronically, which makes revisions a dream: no more tedious retypes. Even before you consider the other advantages of word processors, such as electronic spell-checkers, this puts the computer well ahead of the typewriter.

<u>Working with a Typewriter</u>

Now for the good news. Because word processors have taken over to such a great extent, you can find first-class electric typewriters at ludicrously low prices. Even the IBM "Golfball" (actually, "Selectric") for many years the ultimate typing machine, can be found in thrift stores: As I was writing this, I saw two or three in good working order, at prices ranging from $39.95 to $59.95. Others were sold "as is," often without a type ball, at prices as low as $8.91. Probably, some of these were good runners!

If you are buying a typewriter, machines like these offer the best possible combination of quality and price. Incidentally, my first electric typewriter was a cheap non-IBM portable with a golfball-type head, and I wore it out in less than eighteen months. I had it rebuilt, and the mechanic advised me to sell it to someone who would not give it the pounding that I do, as it would probably be worn beyond repair inside another year if I continued to put the same volume of work through it. I gave it to my sister-in-law, who (when I last checked) was still using it ten years later for light domestic work, and even for preparing lectures (she teaches accountancy), without having any more trouble. I replaced it with a Smith-Corona heavy-duty portable, which was not nearly as pretty, but which was still working perfectly well when I gave it away after four years: I had switched to the computer completely by then.

Manual Typewriters

Manual typewriters are not worth considering, unless you are offering a **very** wide range of other secretarial and clerical services, so that typing is a comparatively minor part of your job. For example, when Patsy acted as my secretary in England, I would not have cared what sort of typewriter she used, as long as it had a clean ribbon. Her skill in dealing with clients, etc., made her so valuable to me that her typing had only to be competent. In fact, it was much better than competent, but that was a bonus!

Three Reasons to Hang on to Your Typewriter

To contradict what I have just said, there are, however, three good reasons for hanging onto your old electric or even manual typewriter, even if you do switch to a computer.

One is for when the computer goes down. While you are waiting for the repairman, you can continue to use your old typewriter; you can use a manual even if the power fails.

Another reason to hang on to (or even buy) an old-fashioned typewriter is that most computer printers cannot do a decent job of addressing an envelope. Unless you want to use stick-on address labels, which do **not** create the same impression as a neatly-typed address on a high-quality envelope, you will still need a typewriter for addressing envelopes. I use my wife's old Olivetti — or maybe I'll go and buy one of those thrift-store "Golfballs" after all!

Lastly, there are few applications that can be filled out on a computer and printer; and it's impossible with a dot matrix printer that has only "tractor feed" (those little spokes that turn around the sides of the typewriter platen [roller] and feed continuous paper through). Fewer and fewer services are interested in doing applications because they are so time-consuming and tedious; here is where you can really make a bundle if you're meticulous and like to make things look good for the sake of making them look good! Professionals filling out job applications want to make a good impression; other individuals may have grant applications they are submitting to a donor company for research and they **must** make a good impression! College students applying to other universities will often submit anywhere from two to five applications to various schools at one time, so you are looking at many hours of typing for just one person. Make no mistake — you *must* do an excellent job, but if you do, word will rapidly spread about your work, and you may become one of the "hot names" in town for doing forms and applications!

2.3   ALTERNATIVES TO CONVENTIONAL TYPEWRITERS

Even if you are not ready, for personal or financial reasons, to move up to a computer (see Chapter 3, "Expanding Your Skills"), there are three compromising options between typewriters and computers.

Buffered Typewriters

The most basic option, after the old-fashioned typewriter, is a "buffered" typewriter. These have a small screen which shows anything up to about three lines of the most recent text: the most limited show only the last sixteen or even eighteen characters, which is *still* better than nothing if you type "nothibg" instead of "nothing" and spot the error in time. It takes a while to get used to the lag between pressing the key and having the letter print out, but you learn soon enough not to worry about it.

Memory Typewriters

The next step up is the "memory typewriter." Again, these have a small screen like a buffered typewriter, but they also store the last few *pages* of text in an electronic memory. This means that you can type something in the usual way, make any necessary corrections, and then reprint the corrected text from memory. These are considerably more expensive than buffered typewriters, though, and they may well be comparable in price with a modestly-priced computer system. Also, once you turn off the typewriter, you lose anything that was in memory — there is no way of storing text electronically in most models.

Word Processing Typewriters

These are like small, specialized computers with a typewriter built in. You can buy these surprisingly cheaply, for as little as $500 or $600, and they are easily the most versatile option after a computer. They are also compact and easy to use, and require no complicated wiring. Their only real drawbacks are first, that they are not quite as versatile as "real" word processors, and second, they are not likely to be fully electronically compatible with your clients' computers; I'll come back to this in the next chapter.

2.4 "CLEANING UP" WORK

You know that the material you are asked to type is not always perfect. I can almost see you smiling when you read that. "Not perfect!" you say. "If only he could see some of the garbage I've been asked to type!"

The difference between working at home and working in an office is that you can't go and ask what on earth Mr. Jones was trying to say when he wrote that, or what Dr. Culpepper's appalling handwriting actually *says*.

By way of experiment, I tried to write "like a doctor": I scribbled the word "chlordiazepoxide" (a tranquillizer, generic Librium) and asked a typist with medical experience to read it. She could tell it was "chlor-something-or-other," but her best guess was "chlordiazerin."

If you simply type a "best guess" like this, the best you can hope for is a retype, and the worst you can do is to kill somebody. I don't know if "chlordiazerin" exists, but for all I (or you) know, it might be a powerful and dangerous drug.

In business, the stakes might not be so high, but your error could be the difference between landing a million-dollar contract and losing it — or more prosaically, between a small businessman making a profit or loss. Of course, everyone makes mistakes, but the more people who are looking out for them, the more chance there is of catching them.

Even then, you cannot bet on your errors being spotted, even if the text is read by dozens of people. Then, the one person who really *matters* will find the mistake. One city legislature recently passed a law providing for **biannual** elections (twice a year) when they thought they were voting for **biennial** elections (once every two years)!

Checking for Errors

So, you need to read through difficult handwritten material *when you get it*, and to mark any specially hard-to-read words, and preferably words you don't understand as well: a fluorescent "highlighter" marker is ideal. Before you start typing, clear up *all* the words you can't read (or understand), and you'll be able to type much faster and more comfortably.

Spelling, Punctuation and Grammar

Another problem lies in the areas of spelling, punctuation, and grammar. You can reasonably assume that a doctor, say, or a professional writer can spell; but what if you are working for a man who has risen from being an auto mechanic to owning his own garage, or a self-made man in the construction business? For that matter, by the time an executive has finished making marginal notes, and crossing out some paragraphs and adding others, he or she may well have lost track of exactly what is on the paper.

Speaking from the other side of the table — someone who hires typists (or used to), rather than typing someone else's work for a living — I can tell you that my favorite typists were the ones who caught every single mistake I made, without trying to "edit" my work. If I had typed "miscellanous" instead of "miscellaneous," my best typists would always catch the mistake; but if they weren't sure about my punctuation, they would always leave it where it was.

The amount of "cleaning up" that you will have to do will inevitably vary from client to client, but it is not a bad idea to discuss this with clients whose work obviously needs it. Some will be very grateful; others will be hostile to the idea. Play it by ear, but if your own education and experience warrant it, don't be afraid to make suggestions. At the other extreme, if you know that your skills are limited to copy-typing, don't get too ambitious!

Reference Books

Regardless of the level of your ambition, there are three or four kinds of reference books that you ought to have. The first and most basic is a good, general dictionary for determining spellings as well as for looking up the meanings of words you don't understand. Rather than buying a small, cheap dictionary for $5.95, go to a used bookstore and get a big, used one — something like Webster's third, or at the very least a Funk and Wagnall. It will cost you anything up to $20, but it will be worth it.

The second is a specialist dictionary for any professional men or women you work with. While legal terms do not change much from year to year (or even decade to decade or century to century for that matter), medical terms change rapidly, so you will need an up-to-date edition if you do medical work. Other clients may suggest specific reference works for their particular requirements.

The third, essential if you plan to type theses and term papers, is something like *Preparing Theses and Other Typed Manuscripts* (Roy O. Billett) or *A Manual for Writers of Term Papers, Theses and Dissertations* by Kate L. Turavian.

The fourth, which is really only important if you want to go beyond copy-typing, is something like Strunk's *The Elements of Style* — a book about the mechanics of writing, and the niceties of writing in English (or at least American; the two languages are more different than you might think). You might also care to buy

The Manual of Style from the University of Chicago Press (commonly known as *The Chicago Style Manual*).

Presentation

"Presentation" has two different meanings. One is concerned with the mechanics of layout, and the other is concerned with the quality of the material you deliver.

Layout

Different people have different layout requirements. There is much more about this in Chapter 5, but the easiest way to see what sort of layout is required is to look at existing material.

Most people who have very specific requirements — such as margin width, two spaces (instead of one) after a comma, and so forth — will issue a "spec sheet" (short for "specification sheet") or typists' guidelines, or even a booklet detailing "house style." Taken in conjunction with a piece of sample material, these can show you exactly what is needed.

Quality

No matter how well you type, even if everything you do is letter-perfect, no one is going to be impressed by your work if it is typed on cheap, nasty paper with a ribbon that is so old and faint that the type is barely readable.

Obviously, a lot depends on what you are typing and who you are typing it for. While a term paper may have very specific *technical* requirements, for example, it can be typed on ordinary 20-lb copier paper with a reasonably fresh fabric ribbon. In case you weren't already aware of it, copier paper (available from any office supply store) is the best way to buy cheap, good quality paper. It is normally sold in reams, strictly 480 sheets but often rounded up to 500 sheets. This is one of the few things in the modern world to be rounded **up** rather than **down!**

Business letters, on the other hand, carry more weight if they are typed on thick, heavy paper with a carbon-film ribbon. Some businesses will supply you with their own preferred, headed paper; that is what I used to do with Patsy. If they *don't* provide paper, you need to have good-quality paper available.

The best place to buy this is usually at a local printer, who will have catalogs of different paper colors, weights, finishes and rag content. They will sell you paper they have in stock or order it for you if they do not have it in stock. High-quality paper will cost a lot more than copier paper, but it will make your letters look much more professional. There may, however, be minimum-order requirements. This may be as low as a ream ($15 to $30, depending on the quality of the paper) or may be as high as $100, so it pays to shop around.

Color — white, or very slightly cream ("off-white") is the most useful color, though you may like to suggest to local businesses that they could use other colors: pale brown or tan is popular, and some companies like pale gray.

Weight — the standard weight for copier paper is "20 lb." Heavier papers, typically 24 lb, may well be used for correspondence. Unfortunately, weight is not a very good guide to the "feel" of a paper, so you need to inspect a sample (and to imagine what it will look like in standard 8½" x 11" letter size) before you buy.

For airmail, it is worth buying a ream of "onion skin" — ultra-lightweight paper that is as thin as its namesake.

Finish — Most paper is "woven"; that is to say, very smooth and flat. If you can detect any texture at all, it is like the weave of a fabric, equally grainy both up-and-down and side-to-side. "Laid" paper has a distinct side-to-side grain, almost like lines running from one side of the paper to the other, and is sometimes favored for high-quality business letters. Many European companies use "laid" paper for their prestige image.

Rag Content — Paper can be made from wood pulp or from rags. *In general*, the higher the rag content of the paper, the tougher it will be and the longer it will last without crisping or browning. High-quality wood-pulp papers are also perfectly acceptable for business letters. For my own correspondence, I use heavy laid white wood-pulp paper, and have done so for many years.

Ribbons — Carbon film ribbons deliver a much cleaner, sharper image than the old-style fabric ribbons. They have to be renewed more often, and can cost anything from $2.50 (from a mail-order discount house) to $10 or more for specialized ribbons bought at full retail. When you consider how much better the carbon-film type looks, though, they are a bargain: you can always charge more for crisp, professional looking work than you can for tired, gray-looking typing.

Your Own Stationery

If you want your own letters to look as good as the ones you do for your clients, you should use high-quality paper and ribbons for these, too. After all, you wouldn't buy a new automobile from a company where the sales lot was full of dirty, uncared-for used cars, would you? The letters you type for clients are your shiny new cars; inquiry letters to your clients, if they are typed on cheap paper with old fabric ribbons, are the equivalent of those old used cars.

2.5 SECRETARIAL SERVICES

A thread which runs through this book is summed up in the repeated phrase, "The more you give, the more you get." The question of providing extra services is dealt with in a number of places, but here we are concerned with a summary of some of your options.

"Covering" for Someone Out-of-Town — As I have already said, this is a very important field for me. I travel a lot, and when I am out of town, I don't want to lose work or to leave urgent mail unanswered. A freelance secretary is invaluable: my mail is redirected to her house, and a message on my answering machine directs calls to her (I suppose I could use "call switching," or "call forwarding").

Photographers, writers, actors, and many others can use a service like this — and if you do a good job for one, his or her friends will surely want to use you.

The pay for this sort of work may not be all that good, but it is interesting and varied and it has the great advantage that you meet all kinds of other people — many of whom may be in a position to give you more work!

Data Entry — If you have a computer, you may well be able to key in "raw" (handwritten) data for all sorts of companies. This is not exciting work, but it can be surprisingly well paid. If your skills lie mainly in fast, accurate copy-typing, this could be ideal for you.

Entering Invoices — Many self-employed people keep their records on the "shoe-box" system. If you can type up a list of all their accounts receivable and payable, on a monthly or even weekly basis, you will be providing an invaluable service.

This will be even more useful if you can enter invoices on a spreadsheet such as Lotus 1-2-3, but there is more about this in the next chapter.

Filing — If you can set up or maintain a filing system which will stop your clients drowning under a sea of paper, they will not only be eternally grateful, they will also pay you for it!

Liaison — A secretary becomes a "personal assistant," with a corresponding rise in prestige and income, when she (or he) takes over some of the work from the boss. If you have clients who trust you enough to say, "Can you call the so-and-so company and chase up our printing order, which seems to be a week late?" you are functioning as a personal assistant — and you can charge a good hourly rate for doing so.

Routine Mail — This is another aspect of being a personal assistant.

You can do it in one of two ways. One is to have your client's business mail delivered to your home, which gives you the chance to weed out junk mail before your client even sees it, and the other is to pick up the mail from your client. Routine business which can be handled like this includes sending out statements and reminder letters, and even preparing checks for your client's signature.

2.6 CONFIDENTIALITY

Even at the very lowest levels of copy-typing, one of the worst business sins you can commit is to fail to respect your clients' confidentiality.

If you are offering secretarial/personal assistant services, you are likely to know a great deal about your clients' business, financial and even personal affairs. You may be surprised to learn that they are running a huge overdraft, or that they are in trouble with the tax man. You may even learn that married clients are having affairs with people to whom they are not married.

Of course, if you find that you are being asked to do things which go against your conscience, or even if you merely wish no longer to work with a particular client, you are free to discontinue your association. If there is clear illegality — for example, if you found incontrovertible evidence that your client was bribing his congressman — you might well feel that it was your duty to go to the police.

What you must NEVER, NEVER do is gossip about your clients, either to your friends or to other clients. If it is known that you cannot be trusted, your career as a freelance typist will be killed stone dead.

2.7 SCHEDULING

The best way to learn how to schedule work is to begin very, very slowly, taking on work only that you are absolutely confident you can deliver on time. Typing term papers is a good example: with (say) a week's deadline, a twenty-page term paper should be well within anyone's capabilities.

Then, you can build up your work as you get a better idea of what you can do. Inevitably, you will make mistakes: there will be times when you wish you had work, but you have not got enough, and there will be others when you have to work longer and harder than you intended; but this is a part of working for yourself.

What you should *not* do is try to plan your days according to a simple formula: fifty words per minute means three thousand words per hour, and you can work (say) five hours a day, so you can do fifteen thousand words. It doesn't work like that. You are not allowing time for interruptions (and there will be interruptions, unless you live on your own in a house with no telephone); for coffee breaks, or for eating; for checking spellings in a dictionary; for trying to read bad handwriting, or work out hard-to-understand passages; or for anything else.

At the very best, a figure that you arrive at in this way should be halved, and then used as a very rough estimate of how much work you can do if you stick to your planned schedule.

The Best Laid Plans

There are two schools of thought about how to plan your time. Both require self-discipline, but they require different kinds of self-discipline, and which you choose will depend on your personality as well as on your personal circumstances.

One school says that you *must* set yourself work hours, and then stick to them: ten in the morning to six at night, say, or from seven in the evening to nine-thirty at night. Even if you have no work, say the proponents of this view, you should sit at your desk and write inquiry letters, practice your typing — anything that will improve your work or your chances of getting it.

The other school says that you can work when you feel like it, and when you fit it in. While this is undoubtedly more fun, it is also very much more dangerous: You decide to call a friend, or go to the shops, or to watch a TV program — and before you know it, your working time is gone. If you don't have too much to do, you can make it up the next day — but if the next day is crowded, too, and if you don't quite get around to working all the hours you intended on that day, either, you can rapidly get further and further behind until you start missing deadlines, and that is the beginning of the end.

In practice, you can to some extent steer a course between these two systems, using the best of both. Either way, you need the discipline to sit down and work, whether you feel like it or not; but the occasional bit of self-indulgence lightens life up, provided you don't do it too often.

The Dangers of Overwork

When the work really starts pouring in, the temptation is to say "Yes!" to everything just to get the money or because you're afraid of losing future business; but this can be self-defeating in two ways.

First, there is sheer overload. If you take on more work than you can handle, everything suffers: your family, your social life, even your friends. You can rapidly become tired and irritable, and the quality of your work begins to suffer.

Second, you may acquire a reputation as someone who never says "No." This results in more and more work, more and more overload, and (once again) a general deterioration of both the quality of your life and the quality of your work. Also, when you are finally forced to say "No," simply because you cannot handle any more work, the clients whose work you refuse may wonder why you are refusing to do their work but accepting everyone else's.

The Schedule Calendar

A notebook-type calendar, with anything from a few lines to a whole page devoted to each day, allows you to make precise notes on who wants what and when; you can also log actual hours spent on each job, each day. This is ideal if the bulk of your work consists of small jobs for different clients, but makes it hard to see long-term deadlines which are days or even weeks away.

A wall-chart planner covers a whole year, and allows you to mark deadlines very easily, so that they can be seen at a glance: I use red self-adhesive stars which can be stuck on and peeled off easily. On the down side, you cannot write detailed notes on a wall-chart, which means that it is more useful if you normally do large jobs with long deadlines. As you can see, neither a notebook nor a wallchart is enough on its own: you really need to use both.

Scheduling Other Parts of Your Life

It may sound weird to talk about "scheduling" time with your friends, family, etc., but unless you do, you may find that your work gets so badly in the way of your social and family life that you wish you had never started. If, for example, you have agreed to take the children out for a pizza, or to go to a movie with your boyfriend/girlfriend/husband/wife/significant other, then log the date in your engagement calendar and don't break it.

This applies on a daily basis as well as on a weekly or "special event" basis. Schedule time to be with the people you live with, whether they are family or friends. Inevitably, their plans and yours will not always coincide, so there will be times when you are free and they are busy, and vice versa; unless you make an attempt to be with them, it is all too easy to become isolated.

2.8   PRICING

I wish I could say this was the $64,000 question, but unfortunately you are unlikely to earn quite that much! Setting a fair price is *extremely* difficult, and it is impossible in a book like this to give actual dollar amounts that you should charge for specific services. There are three reasons why this is so.

The first is geographical. If you are near the center of New York City, or handy for Hollywood, you may well be able to charge two or even three times as much as someone in a small Midwestern or Southern town.

The second is skill-related. If you are a copy typist, pure and simple, and have only a typewriter instead of a computer, then obviously you cannot charge as much as someone who offers a full range of secretarial services including word processing and electronic spreadsheets.

The third is personal. If you already enjoy a good business relationship with someone — your former employer, say — then you can charge more than if you are a complete stranger. This is why established "temp" agencies can charge as much as they do: their reputation is worth real money.

There are (and always have been) two ways of working out prices. Technically, they are known as "product-oriented" and "market-oriented."

Product-Oriented Pricing

This looks at what it costs to make a product or to provide a service — in your case, the price of paper, depreciation on the typewriter, the value you place on your time, etc. — and then adds a percentage mark-up for profit. Product-oriented pricing is (as its name suggests) more useful when you are a widget manufacturer than when you are offering a service, but you can use it to work out roughly how *little* you can afford to work for.

For example, if you offer a pick-up and delivery service, you are going to have to maintain an automobile, and to pay for the gas. Don't say, "But I've got an automobile anyway"; you have to allow for the *extra* gas, the *extra* wear and tear, and so forth, in working out your expenses. Likewise, think of your telephone bill. It will almost inevitably be higher than it used to be, even if you don't put in a special business line (see Chapter 6, "Coping with Success").

All your figures will be guesstimates, but if you work out your monthly expenditure, and then divide it by the number of hours you plan to work, you can arrive at a dollars-per-hour figure that you *must* earn in order to cover your costs.

This sort of exercise is especially important if you are thinking of renting an office or buying extra equipment (Chapter 6 again). Suppose you plan to work about 25 hours a week, 100 hours a month. If you are paying rent of $200 a month, this means you will have to add $2 per hour to your hourly rate just to pay the rent! Likewise, a $600 fax machine on 12 months interest-free credit is $50 a month — another $.50 an hour just to pay for the machine, though obviously you would not buy the fax unless you thought it was going to earn money for you. The following checklist will help you to work out your expenses.

MONTHLY EXPENSES

Paper, envelopes, etc.	$_____
Ribbons and other supplies	$_____
Postage	$_____
Telephone	$_____
Heat and Utilities (even at home!)	$_____
Gasoline	$_____
Other Automobile Expenses	$_____
Advertising (see Chapter 4)	$_____
Business Licenses, Etc. (Chapter 6)	$_____
Rent	$_____
Payments for Office Equipment	$_____
_____	$_____
_____	$_____
_____	$_____
_____	$_____
_____	$_____
MONTHLY TOTAL	$_____
MINIMUM NUMBER OF HOURS YOU EXPECT TO WORK EACH MONTH	_____

Divide the number of hours into the monthly total to get your expenses per hour. If they are under about $1.50, and certainly if they are under $1, think again: are you being totally honest about what it is going to cost you to work for yourself? If they are over about $3, look at ways of saving money — do you really **need** to rent an office?

To your expenses-per-hour figure, add $5: this gives you the *minimum* you can afford to charge. This is not much more than minimum wage, and if you are going to have the hassles of running your own business, you certainly don't want to work for $2 per hour!

Market-Oriented Pricing

This looks at what other people are charging for the same sort of work, and then cuts the coat to suit the cloth. If "temp" agencies in your area are charging $12 an hour, this means they are paying the people who work for them about $6.50 an hour: it may be as much as $7.50, or it may be as little as $6, but you can normally reckon that a person the agency sends out gets about half what the agency charges.

In order to find out what other people charge, you can do one of three things.

First, you can call temp agencies to find out what they charge: Pretend that you are someone's secretary, and that you are just calling around on behalf of your boss in order to get prices. Describe the kind of work **you** want to do — "we're looking for someone to type up contracts" — and ask how much they would charge per hour.

Second, ask any business contacts you have (including friends-of-friends, and husbands-of-friends) what their business pays temp agencies.

Third, call the temp agency and ask them what they would pay you, if you were working for them as a temp. *Don't* ask them what they charge their clients! You know that they will add on a mark-up of approximately 100%, so you have a good idea of what they would charge a client for your time.

Getting in the Ballpark

Once you know roughly what the agencies charge, you can work out roughly what you should charge. You can do one of two things. Either you can undercut them slightly, or you can offer a better service for the same money (or you can even charge more).

The undercutting may be necessary because the big agencies already have excellent reputations, and many employers may decide that if it's a question of giving $12.50 an hour to the big agency or $12.50 to you, they'll stick with the big company. They'll switch to you if you can offer an equal service for less money — but they won't expect it to be *much* less, because they know that you, they and Kelly Girl are all in business to make a profit. If you split the difference between the agencies' charging rate (to the client) and the agencies' paying rate (to the typist), most clients will reckon that the price is fair.

Of course, some people may be willing to pay **more** than they would pay a temp agency (or at least to pay as much) if you can offer a service which is better tailored to their needs. For example, a movie company that needed scripts typed on a "rush" basis might well be willing to pay over the odds if they knew you would work far into the night to deliver it for them. Typing until two or three in the morning may not be much fun, and it may not be something you'd want to do on a regular basis, but $20 an hour makes it much more attractive!

The Basic Ballpark Figure

If you want a ballpark figure, right now — and you would have every right to feel cheated if a book such as this did not give you one — your starting point should be $10 an hour.

Knock dollars off if you live in a small town where wages are typically low, and knock dollars off if your skills are limited: If you live in (say) rural Mississippi or West Virginia, and can offer only copy-typing, you might be very lucky to get $6.50 an hour.

Add dollars on if you live in a city where secretarial skills are much in demand, or if you can offer extra skills such as spreadsheets (page 57). If you are *really* good (and *really* lucky), and you live next door to an advertising studio or a movie production company, $15 an hour might be too low!

Don't Overcharge — or Undercharge

Most of us are so worried about overcharging that we set our prices too low. The risk is obvious: if your prices are too high, no one is going to be willing to pay them.

At the other end of the scale, though, you can get into just as much trouble by charging too little. The big problems are these:

First, if your prices are too low, some people may be afraid to hire you because they are afraid you are no good. Imagine you are in the market for a used automobile, and you know that the going rate for the one you want is $3000. At $2700, or even $2400, you might think you were getting a bargain. But if someone was asking only $1900, you would immediately wonder what was wrong with it!

Second, if you get a reputation for working too cheaply, you will find it very difficult to ever raise your prices. You will be stuck at the bottom end of the market. This could also attract clients who don't care what's fair to you, as long as their work is done *cheaply*; no matter how little you charge, to them it will always be "too much." These same clients will constantly ask for "favors" which they don't expect to pay for!

Third, why earn less than you could? Say you charge $8 an hour when you could charge $12 an hour. This means that for a 100-hour month, you earn only $800 instead of $1200; or alternatively, if you are content with $800 a month, you could earn it in 67 hours instead of in 100!

2.9   WHEN TO EXPECT PAYMENT

As anyone in a small business will tell you, bad debts can be a problem. A "bad debt" is where someone owes you money and just doesn't pay. A particularly depressing form of bad debt is when someone commissions work, then never even collects it, let alone pays for it. If you have just typed a 300-page novel, this is terrible!

How you charge your customers will, however, depend on how well you know them and on what sort of work you do for them. There are three main options: split payments, payment on delivery, and payment on account.

Split Payments

Split payments are the best way to deal with big jobs or new customers. Usually, you ask for half when you accept the job, and half when you deliver it. For a $200 job, therefore, you would ask for $100 "up front."

A variation on this is the deposit. This is useful if you are not sure what the final bill is going to be. For example, if you are charging (say) $10 per hour and know you can type eight double-spaced pages per hour, you may not know how many pages the novel will turn out to be; you might ask for $150 or $200 as a deposit, with the balance on delivery. You might even go for stage payments: delivery in 40-page batches (5 hours), with $50 down and the balance in full at the end of each section.

Payment on Delivery

With established customers, and relatively small amounts (up to $20), this may be more convenient for your customers. Of course, it is less convenient for you, but you increase your prices by a dollar an hour to compensate for this ....

Payment on Account

With well-established customers for whom you do a *lot* of small jobs, you may both find it more convenient to establish some sort of weekly or even monthly billing system. Bi-weekly billing is preferable, as people may get a bit of a shock when they see how much they are paying you every month, although it's more common practice to bill on a monthly basis. The interval can be worked out with your clients, although it's best to be consistent and not have a separate billing time for each client. You'll find that adding up time and billing *does* take a good deal of your time, so you'll want to do as much as you can at one time.

2.10   NEVER SPEND YOUR OWN MONEY!

If you are doing any sort of job that requires you to lay out money — paying printers, or buying advertising space, or doing anything else that your client should pay for, *get the money up front*. NEVER spend your own money, even if you are working for an old friend.

2.11 SPEED, QUALITY AND PRICE

I began this chapter by saying that <u>speed</u> comes second to <u>quality</u>. The great news is, if you can offer **both** speed and quality, price comes third in the eyes of most clients!

Obviously, this depends on where you are and what sort of work you do, but there will be times when people want work done on a super-rush basis (advertising agencies call these jobs "screamers"), and they don't really care what they pay, as long as the work is done perfectly and on time. If you can work with firms who regularly have "screamers," you may well be able to charge $20 and $30 an hour for five- or ten-hour jobs. In order to do this, though, you have to be *good*, and you have to know **where to look**; and these are the subjects of the next two chapters.

3.0 <u>EXPANDING YOUR SKILLS</u>

At the beginning of the book, I said that "keyboard skills" was the fashionable new phrase for being able to type — but really, there's a lot more to it than that. If you can already touch-type, you can use *any* standard keyboard. It doesn't really matter whether that keyboard is connected to a typewriter, a telex machine, a computer or a purpose-built word processor. There is no reason, therefore, to be afraid of these new machines: you already possess the basic skill that you need in order to use them.

Of course, you do need to learn some more skills in order to get the most out of the new technology. In theory, you could probably copy-type onto a computer keyboard without knowing anything whatsoever about the computer — it really is that simple — but if you are going to *use* the computer, you need to know what it can do.

So: how do you learn about word processing and other keyboard applications? First, you read this chapter. Once you have read the next few pages, you will know whether you want to learn more — and then, at the end of the chapter, there is more information on *how* to learn more, whether from books, from courses at local colleges, or from temp agencies.

3.1 <u>WHAT IS WORD PROCESSING?</u>

With a typewritten text, the only ways of making changes are mechanical. You can erase or white-out parts, and type over them; you can change the order of the pages; or with scissors and a glue-pot (or stapler), you can rearrange the order of individual paragraphs. You can also make hand-written notes in the text or in the margin.

Needless to say, none of this improves the appearance of the text. No doubt, you have had to re-type work that has been hacked about in this way, just to make it look presentable — and if it is (say) a 20-page document, this means 20 pages of retyping.

A word processor allows you to make <u>all</u> these changes electronically: corrections, re-orderings, "take-ins", and everything else. In fact, the facility for moving blocks of text around — anything from a sentence (or even a word) to a paragraph or a chapter — is sometimes known as "electronic cut-and-paste."

The real magic is that you need *only* to re-type the bits that need changing. Even a totally butchered text rarely has more than ten per cent of the text altered, and with a word processor, that is the ten percent you re-type. With a conventional typewriter, you have to re-type the other ninety percent as well, just to make the whole thing look presentable. Obviously, the savings in time — and the potential for really superb quality — are enormous!

Word Processors And Computers

Almost any reasonably powerful computer — in other words, anything more than a toy or games-only computer — can run word-processing programs. This book was written on a Sharp PC45101 portable using WordStar Version 4.0. My "big" computer (which is only bigger physically — actually it is older and less powerful) is a Philips P2000C running WordStar Version 3.3.

Sometimes, though, you may encounter "dedicated" word-processors, which are computers specially set up to run a particular word processing (WP) program. While these are a little more convenient, because the "function" keys are specially marked with such symbols as "Format Paragraph" or "End of Line," they are usually more expensive (unless you buy an obsolete system) and they are no more versatile. Also, you may have difficulty in running spreadsheets on them.

3.2   COMPUTER SYSTEMS

Most people who were brought up with typewriters HATE computers when they are first introduced to them. There seems to be so much to learn; you don't have a reassuring piece of paper with words on it; and (perhaps worst of all) there are all those horror stories about computers failing and "losing" days or even weeks of work.

Well, these drawbacks are very real: there's no doubt about that. On the other hand, the advantages are so enormous that you can learn to live with the disadvantages — and besides, the disadvantages are not as serious as they seem. Learning to use a really comprehensive word processing program represents two or three weeks of pure hell, when you will feel like putting your foot through the screen and hurling the machine across the room. At least, that's how long it took me; if you are already "computer literate," it may take you much less time. But once you've learned it, running WordStar on a computer is just as easy as using a typewriter — in fact, in many ways, it's easier.

Not having "hard copy" (computer jargon for "words on paper") is something you quickly learn to live with, and it saves you from disappearing under mountains of old drafts. Of course, if you want mountains of old drafts (or if you are paranoid about losing stuff that exists only on disk), you can always print them out at the end of every day, or even as you finish each document.

As for "losing" work — well, if you save your work to disk every few minutes, and make back-up copies, the risk is slight and you should never irretrievably lose more than a few minutes work unless a disk is physically destroyed, which is about as likely as spilling coffee across a pile of typing. Even then, your back-up disk will mean that you never lose more than a day's work, even if the dog eats the disk just as you're preparing to finish for the day. Don't worry about the terms "save to disk" and "make back-up copies": I'll explain them shortly.

Now, let's look at the real positive advantages.

Why Word Processing Is The Wave Of The Future

First, as I have already said, corrections are a breeze. This is true whether you are correcting a three-paragraph letter, or a three-hundred-page book manuscript. Instead of retyping whole pages, you just correct the letter, word or phrase — even paragraph — that is wrong. Using "electronic cut-and-paste," you can move sentences, paragraphs, whole pages. The computer takes care of re-aligning ("reformatting") the paragraphs, and the printer takes the drudgery out of typing a new copy.

Second, you can set up standard text (often known as "boilerplate") for standard letters, bills, contracts, and the like. If you habitually work with the same people, you can just fill in the blanks on the "boilerplate." The savings in time are enormous, and you are freed from drudge-work. The time you save can, of course, be used to earn money!

Third, the quality of the final work is a dream: no more white-out fluid, erasures, or hand-written corrections. Every line is perfect.

Fourth, you can make all sorts of changes to the physical appearance of the document with the very minimum of effort. You want narrower margins? Shorter pages? Boldface? No problem: a few simple key-strokes can take care of them all.

Finally, you don't really need to know very much about computers. I don't even like computers, but I use them all the time. Once you have mastered a few bits of jargon and got your system up and running, you can treat the computer in exactly the same way that you treated your typewriter: as a straightforward, reliable tool which you use without thinking about it. Except, of course, that it is vastly more powerful than your old typewriter, both in what it can do and (most important of all) in what it can earn for you.

3.3 A LITTLE BIT OF JARGON

In order not to be **too** bewildered by computer salesmen, you need to know a few words of jargon. These are easy to learn, and if you understand them, you need not be worried about being blinded with (pseudo) science. Besides, if you get the kind of salesman that tries to show off his knowledge at your expense, you're dealing with the wrong man: you want someone whose aim is to help you, not to show off!

Hardware and Software

"Hardware" is the computer itself, and its accessories (computer people call accessories "peripherals"), while "software" is what you use the computer for — WordStar, for example, is a piece of word-processing software. "Software" is also commonly referred to as "programs."

Not all software will run on all hardware, though standardization is steadily increasing. Basically, there are three "families" of hardware and software: IBM, Apple/Macintosh and CP/M (see below).

IBM Compatible Computers and "Operating Systems"

Almost all modern computers conform to the standard set by IBM, and are, therefore, called IBM-compatible. The other main "standard" is set by Apple/Macintosh. Guess what: these machines are called Macintosh-compatible.

In order to control the information they are processing, IBM-compatible machines use an "operating system" called PC-DOS, which is very like the MS-DOS (MicroSoft Disk Operating System) used by IBM compatibles.

Some machines use other systems: Apple/Macintosh have their own system (AppleDOS), and older machines use CP/M (Control Program/Microprocessors). Some Radio Shack machines use TRSDOS. I use both CP/M and MS-DOS machines impartially: they all do what I want, which is what *you* want too!

Memory and Speed

Memory is one measure of the power of a computer – it is a bit like the horsepower of a car. Just as a 250-horsepower car is more powerful than a 100-horsepower car, so a 512K computer is more powerful than a 64K computer.

The "K" stands for "Kilobytes." It doesn't matter exactly what a Kilobyte is. After all, how accurately could you define a horsepower?

Remember that just as you don't need an Indianapolis race car to take the children to school, you don't need a superpowerful computer to run word processing programs. I'll come back to this later.

"Speed," as applied to computers, is very misleading. Different people tell you that their machines run at "this many Hertz" (abbreviated Hz) or "that many Hertz," but it doesn't seem to make that much difference to how well (or how badly) they run a word-processing program. This is where you hear numbers like "3086," which apply to what sort of microchips your machine uses. I don't know how fast my machines run (in Hertz) and I don't care, but I do know that my Philips runs WordStar faster than my Sharp, but that Lotus 1-2-3 on the Sharp is both faster and more powerful than the old CalcStar on my Philips.

One last thing on speed is 8-bit, 16-bit and 32-bit machines. This is a very technical matter that refers to how computers handle information, and 8-bit is plenty fast enough for any application described in this book. More modern machines are 16-bit, and "state-of-the-art" is 32-bit — but you don't need to worry about any of this.

Disk Drives

In order to run programs, and to save your work electronically, your computer must have disk drives. These accept square envelopes which contain a disk (called the "floppy disk" or just "floppy") which records the programs and your work. It is coated with a magnetic medium like that found on recording tape.

Floppies get smaller all the time. The old floppies were eight inches across; then they went to 5¼ inches; and the most modern floppies are 3½ inches in diameter. Both 5¼ inch and 3½ inch are in common use; don't bother with an eight-inch machine.

Each floppy can hold a certain amount of information, and this is again measured in Kilobytes (K). Most 5¼ inch disks hold either 360K or 720K; most 3½ disks hold 720K, though more and more hold 144K (also known as 1.44 MB, for *Megabytes* — or "million-bytes").

Extra disk capacity is useful. If you have 720K drives, you can run your word processing program, with all its bells and whistles such as spell checkers and an electronic thesaurus, in one drive and your working disk in the other, and the only time you will need to change disks is when you make back-up copies (see below). A twin-disk machine is only just adequate to run an older, basic word processing program; if you intend to keep up with the industry and employ the updated versions of your old programs, you *MUST* get a machine with a hard disk that has at least 20MB. Computers known as "XT" are quickly being replaced by faster machines with more memory (150 MB is not uncommon!); however, they are perfect if you are only using one to four programs, and the prices are becoming ridiculously affordable. They are going the way of the transistor radio: once very expensive ($20-$30 back in the 1960's) to $9.95 for something that works even better than the original. The XT computer is simply not on the "cutting edge" anymore, so even though it would be ideal for *your* (and my) needs, it's not in big demand and doesn't cost much.

Saving to Disk — While you are typing a file, the work is being stored in the machine's memory. In order to save it in permanent form, you need to record it on the disk. If the power fails, you will lose all the work you did since the last "save." This is why it is a good idea to save your work to disk every few minutes. It is very easy: you usually press two keys, and thirty seconds later, the work is safely recorded magnetically.

Back-up — If your disk is destroyed, for example by sticky fingers or a spilled cup of coffee, you can forget about ever using it again. For this reason, you should always "back up" at the end of the day. This means making an identical copy of your work disk.

There are several ways of doing a backup, but the easiest is simply to make copies of your floppy disk files onto another floppy disk. In IBM format, this is done with a "DISKCOPY" command to the computer which walks you through, step by step, once the command has been properly given.

If you are using a hard disk and keep your client files there, you will not have to be constantly switching floppy disks in and out all day (since you will probably keep separate disks for your various clients). Working from the hard disk is more time efficient and much easier; it also makes backing up much easier and quicker. There are many *extremely* easy back-up programs available which, once you start them, walk you through the steps with choices you pick from the screen. Although working from a hard disk is usually preferable to working from floppy, you really must faithfully do your backup, because if the disk were to "crash" (get destroyed), then you will have irretrievably lost ALL information stored on it. Obviously this could be more of a catastrophe than simply losing one floppy disk, but if you have consistently backed up your files, you will have nothing to worry about.

A third possibility is a "streaming tape backup"; this is a sophisticated and quite expensive alternative. It's only real saving grace is that it is extremely fast. However, your need for "extremely fast" will only surface when you have a hard disk with 60 MB or more, which could take quite a lot of time to back up onto floppy disks. For now, it's enough that you know they exist, but you certainly shouldn't be talked into purchasing something like this unless you're simply into having the latest and best technology!

3.4   CHOOSING A COMPUTER

If you are not "computer literate," there is no doubt that computers are intimidating. Matters are often made worse by computer "experts" who dazzle you with RAM, ROM, 640K, 3086, DOS and all kinds of other jargon, and who assure you that you need an insanely complicated (and expensive) computer system that will do everything.

Fortunately, you can ignore nine-tenths of it — or more. Once you have absorbed the little bit of jargon listed above, you need to know three things:

1.   Do you like the keyboard?

2.   Is the screen comfortably visible?

3.   Can it run the programs (software) you need?

Keyboard choice certainly requires no special training. As a skilled typist, you will know which keyboards feel right, and which ones feel rubbery, imprecise, or otherwise awkward. This is *totally* personal, so don't be talked into a "better" keyboard that doesn't feel right *to you.*

Likewise, screen visibility is easy to determine. If you are not comfortable with it, ask to see a different one. Some screens are green, some are amber, and some are white-on-black, while others are black-on-white. You don't *need* a color monitor, although if you will be typing long hours, they are generally easier on your eyes. And, of course, they're much more fun!

As for the third question, about running the programs you need, you can run the *older* versions of industry standards, but this will limit your compatibility with your clients. Most people who like the program they are using will install the updated versions as they come out; and the updated versions typically use more and more computer memory. Keep this in mind when purchasing a computer; if your software takes up every bit of the computer's memory when you start out, you will likely need more in no time at all. If you aren't worried about keeping up with your clients, and your programs do all you'll ever want them to do, fine. But it's the rare self-employed business person who doesn't constantly think of ways to get better and offer more services (and make more money)!

You can buy a perfectly satisfactory new computer from a local dealer for under $1000.00, and if you look through a magazine called *COMPUTER SHOPPER* (available at any bookstore), you can find all kinds of discount deals. In fact, during the twelve months before this book went to press, I saw two desperate firms offering two separate word processing systems complete with computer, software and printer for under $500. Remember what I said earlier about the "XT" type of machines ... once a computer is no longer a "leading edge" machine, the real "computer junkies" ignore them and the rest of us can buy them at *great* prices!

If you take the mail-order route, though, make sure that you have a computer-knowledgeable friend to help you set your system up. Stores provide a degree of "hand-holding" which is simply *not available* over the telephone.

No matter where you buy, you should also check guarantees — how long they are, and what they cover — and where the machine can be serviced. If the machine has to be returned to Japan for servicing, you are in trouble when it breaks down (and it *will*, at some point)!

3.5   PRINTERS

Like computers, it is easy to be intimidated by printers; again, there's a lot of jargon: daisywheel, dot-matrix, letter quality (often abbreviated to LQ), near letter quality (NLQ), laser...

Again, like computers, you don't need to understand much of it. Better still, the best choice for anyone offering a typing service is likely to be one of the cheapest options: the daisywheel printer.

Daisywheels

Basically, a daisywheel operates on a similar sort of principle to an IBM Selectric, though simpler. The letters are all arranged on the spokes of a rimless wheel. If you have a strong enough imagination, it looks a bit like a flower with lots of long, thin petals — hence "daisywheel."

The wheel spins, and when the right letter or character is in place, a little hammer smacks it against the paper. The result is typewriter-quality printing; you even have the choice (as with typewriters) of fabric ribbons or carbon-film ribbons. You should always use carbon-film ribbons for the beautifully crisp, clear image they give on the paper. The daisywheels also come in a large variety of typestyles, so you can add italics and decorative scripts, big bold letters, etc.

By modern standards, daisywheel printers are <u>slow</u>: they can take a minute or more to print a whole page of single-spaced text. To anyone brought up on typewriters, this is still pretty amazing! The more money you spend, the faster the print speed: The cheapest daisy-wheels cost $200.00 or less from the discount merchants, and type 15 to 20 characters per second (cps), while the most expensive cost $600.00 or more and type at up to to 80 cps. I use a modestly-priced daisy wheel as the best possible compromise on value and quality.

Dot Matrix

These are responsible for those awful things you sometimes see where the letter is made up of lots of miserable little dots. The great advantage of a dot matrix printer in "draft mode" (which is when it prints out those dotty letters) is that it is fast: speeds of 50-100 cps are regarded as slow, 100-200 cps as normal, and over 200 cps as nothing unusual.

If the dot matrix printer offers "letter quality" (LQ) or "near letter quality" (NLQ), it uses <u>more</u> dots to create a better-quality letter. In doing so, the speed drops dramatically: some NLQ printers are as slow as daisy-wheels when they are used in this way. Only you can tell if such a printer does, in fact, offer adequate quality for your clients. Some people refer to "NLQ" as "correspondence quality," but I wouldn't like to receive a letter written that way! Additionally, many dot matrix printers are set up to use continuous-form paper that you have to tear apart at the perforations (on four sides!), and feeding high-quality stationery through them can be, at the very least, a hassle. All things considered, unless you intend to also purchase a daisy-wheel printer for your "final product," or if you foresee doing a LOT of graphics, charts, etc., this is certainly *not* the preferred type of printer for you to spend your hard-earned money on. Often clients will make their decision of who to take the work to based on what type of printer you have. After all, the final product is what they are paying for, and if it doesn't look good, it doesn't matter how good you are at everything else.

A good, reasonably fast dot-matrix printer costs between $200.00 and $500.00, though you can easily pay more. If you pay less, it is likely to be as slow as a daisywheel when it is used in LQ or NLQ mode, and has to offer no real advantages.

Laser

Laser printers offer two big advantages and two big disadvantages. Taking the advantages first:

The first advantage is that you can choose a wide variety of typefaces and sizes, and the quality is superb: it is all but indistinguishable from typesetting. These are the machines used for so-called "desk-top publishing." They are also wonderful for printing graphics, which most good word processing programs and spreadsheet programs now support.

The second advantage is that they are *fast:* six or eight pages per minute is normal. They are also very quiet, usually with a noise level equal to or less than a photocopier.

The first disadvantage is that they are expensive: the cheapest Hewlett-Packard laser printer (the standard in the industry) is well over $1000, and the better models approach $2000. You can easily pay more than this for top-of-the-line models.

The second disadvantage is that they use the same technology as photocopiers, and when they fail, they cost as much as photocopiers to fix (but in all fairness, they are generally highly reliable). Lasers do not use ribbons; they use toner cartridges which are very similar to those you put in photocopiers. These cartridges can be expensive, but there are alternatives to buying new cartridges (such as having the old ones refilled), and you can print approximately 3,000 pages per cartridge!

To sum up, they allow you to do things that no other printer can begin to do, but you need to invest a lot more money in buying one, and, of course, more time in learning all the wonderful things it can do. Once again, only you can decide whether they are worth the extra money (and time) to you.

It is worth knowing, though, that *some* instant-print shops and even some computer stores will let you hire their laser printers on an hourly basis: Typical costs run between $5.00 and $15.00 an hour, plus a per-sheet cost for what you actually print. You bring your disk in, with the text all ready to print, and you can print a great deal of text in even half an hour (the normal minimum charge period). Of course, your system must be compatible with theirs, so you will need to discuss this with them.

3.6   CONNECTING COMPUTERS TO PRINTERS

Unfortunately, this is not just a matter of buying the right cable and connecting the two: you normally have to "configure" the software to make the best use of the printer. The manual normally tells you (fairly) clearly how to do this, but you can still reckon on a day or two of some frustration while you get everything set up. Once again, a computer-literate friend will smooth the path greatly.

Buffers Or Spoolers

These are two different names for a device (which may be an external piece of hardware or an internal piece of software) which allows you to print at the same time that you are editing on the screen. On older machines, the computer could not be used to edit while printing, which is obviously a major drawback.

For example, while I was writing these words, my printer was printing out the previous chapter. Without some kind of buffer or spooler, this would not be possible. In fact, I have two external buffers for the big, old Philips machine, and an internal spooling program ("background print") is built into WordStar Release 4, which is what I run on the Sharp.

Some printers have buffers built in; you need at least 8K for most realistic uses. My buffers are 16K and 64K, respectively.

3.7   WORD PROCESSING PROGRAMS

Exactly which word-processing program you choose is up to you. Each has its advantages and disadvantages, in terms of speed, versatility, and ease of learning.

It is a good idea to inquire among your clients and prospective clients which system they use so that your software is fully compatible with theirs. The example I have used in this book is WordStar, because that is what I use and what I know, but you should be aware that there are *many* others such as *Microsoft Word*, *Applewriter*, *WordPerfect* and *Word Plus*. If your clients all use different systems, WordPerfect is probably the closest to industry standard — the best mixture of versatility, ease of use, and general acceptability. The next most popular program is probably Microsoft Word.

WordPerfect's main advantage is that compared with some systems, it is fairly easy to learn; and once you have learned it, you have a tremendously powerful package at your fingertips. Also, you don't have to learn all about WordPerfect at once; you can use a few basic features almost instantly, almost as easily as you currently type, and then learn to use the other features as you need them.

It would probably be a good idea for you to do some quick research in your area to see what would be the most useful program for you to purchase: Use the Yellow Pages, call the other secretarial services and simply ask them what word processing programs they use; no explanation of why you are calling is necessary. Alternatively, call some of the offices of businesses you want to target (law firms, for example) and ask them the same question. If 90% of the answers are one particular program, your choice is probably obvious.

Spell Check

Most word processing programs now include a spellcheck feature, which you will not want to be without unless you will never type long documents. The spellcheck will stop at all words it doesn't know and ask you whether it's correct, usually giving you a list of alternative words (handy if you're not the world's best speller yourself!). Additionally, the spellchecker can be "educated"; that is, if you regularly use particular names or words that your speller doesn't know, you can add the names and words to it, and it will never bother you with them again!

Buying Word Processing Programs

Sometimes you will get a word processing program as part of a package deal when you buy a computer. If it's a good program, great: you've just saved anything from $150.00 (the cheapest WP programs, discounted) to $500.00 or more (full list price — which almost *no one* ever pays). If it is not a very versatile system, or if it is a very little-used system, you may want to buy a "real" word processing program instead. Again, remember that compatibility with clients can sometimes get (or lose) jobs.

It's worth knowing, though, that once you are a "registered user" of many systems, you can buy updated versions of the same program quite cheaply. For example, my original WordStar came free with my Philips computers; but for $90.00 or so, I was able to update to the latest version when I bought my new MS-DOS machine.

3.8 SPREADSHEET PROGRAMS

Anyone who has ever had anything to do with accounting will know what a spreadsheet looks like: row upon row of figures in columns. It needn't be accounting, either: when a teacher has a row of pupils' names, and the marks they got in different tests, it is still a spreadsheet. For example, a school record might look like this:

								AVERAGE
Allinson, A	50	55	43	28	33	48	65	46
Bogdanovich, M	67	78	75	66	70	80	79	74
Corby, X	65	93	63	74	95	60	83	76

and from this you can see that Anne Allinson has trouble with her grades; Martin Bogdanovich is a competent sort of student; while Xerxes Corby can do very well when he wants, but doesn't always bother. If you think about it, what is a report card other than a spreadsheet?

Likewise, a simple accounting example might look like this:

	1988	1989	1990
Telephone	600	800	850
Postage	150	200	250
Utilities	600	500	700
Stationery	200	250	300
TOTAL EXPENSES	1550	1750	2100
GROSS INCOME	2500	4000	5500
GROSS PROFIT	950	2250	3400

You can see how figures like these might apply to your own typing business! You can also see that while expenses are rising, income is rising faster, so your profits are getting bigger.

Calculating With Spreadsheets

Although spreadsheets of all kinds are a convenient way of collecting, organizing and showing information, you often need to do calculations as part of the spreadsheet. In the accounting example, you had to add together the different kinds of expenses to arrive at the total; while in the school example, you could average out marks to see what each pupil can do.

Although you <u>can</u> do this with a pencil, a sheet of accounting paper and a calculator, a spreadsheet program makes it a good deal easier — it can add together all the numbers in a given row or column, and then average them or do anything else you want. It can represent the information as a bar-chart or pie-chart, if you have the right sort of printer (dot matrix or laser).

In fact, spreadsheets are enormously powerful tools that are used by all kinds of people every day — but what has this to do with running your own typing business?

Offering Spreadsheet Services

The answer is simple. If you know how to set up a spreadsheet using a spreadsheet program such as Lotus 1-2-3, Microsoft Works, Excel, etc., and how to enter numbers into it, you are offering people a *very attractive* service. As I have already said, many professional people and small businessmen keep their records on the "shoe-box" principle, and if you can take their receipts, etc., out of the shoe box (or wherever else they store them) and file them neatly in date order *and* enter them on a spreadsheet, you will be doing work that they would otherwise have to pay an accountant a minimum of $30.00 an hour (and possibly a lot more) to do. See the advantages?

You **don't** have to understand all the things that a spreadsheet can do in order to be able to offer such a service. At the most basic, all you have to be able to do is set the spreadsheet up and enter the numbers. You really should be able to do simple totals as well. That's it! If your clients can take your spreadsheets (preferably on disk as well), and give these to their accountants, their accountants can do all the "number-crunching" that is necessary.

Spreadsheets And Taxes

With a spreadsheet program, you can set up a table where the vertical columns correspond to the IRS tax form headings such as Meals, Travel, Repairs, Office Expenses, Automobile Expenses, Publications, and so forth. The rows are each individual receipts: date, company, dollar amount, and then the dollar amount "spread" to be under the relevant heading. A very simplified example, with only some of the headings, might look like this:

DATE	COMPANY	EXPENSE	AMOUNT	AUTO-MOBILE	UTIL/PHONE	OFFICE EXPS.	MEALS
11/1	Johnson	Lunch	32.64				32.64
11/1	U.S.P.S.	Postage	5.65			5.65	
11/1	Chevron	Gas	13.00	13.00			
11/1	Bell	Phone	164.13		164.13		
11/2	Federal Express	Parcel	3.19			3.19	
11/2	OfficeWld	Paper	14.53			14.53	
TOTALS			233.14	13.00	164.13	23.37	32.64

You can even check that everything is correctly entered by cross-adding the spread numbers ($13.00, $164.13, $23.37 and $32.64) to make sure that they add up to $233.14. The spreadsheet program will, of course, do this for you!

The 1040 Long Form and Schedule C should tell you all you need to know about setting up spreadsheets of this type. Offering a service like this will *really* save your clients both time and money, and (of course) you can also use it for your own taxes!

Buying A Spreadsheet Program

The reason I have referred to Lotus 1-2-3 is simple: because it is the industry standard. Even if people don't buy Lotus 1-2-3, they look for a program that is Lotus 1-2-3 "compatible" — that is, which can use information in Lotus 1-2-3 format. There are other programs, but unless they are 1-2-3 compatible, you may be offering your clients a much less valuable service.

3.9 DATABASES

A database program is one that contains a lot of information — "data" — and provides various ways of getting the information out. The most obvious example of a database is a mailing list, such as a list of a firm's customers, or a doctor's clients. At the simplest, you could "access" (get out) the information by looking up every name, or every name beginning with "B."

More sophisticated databases contain more information. For example, you might be able to "access" all the people on the list who are aged over 21, or who live in certain zip-code areas.

There is no point in giving more information about databases here, but it is worth knowing that database programs exist — and if you get into mailing lists (Chapter 5), you might just want to use one. Another example that I have heard of was someone who set up a database of dog pedigrees — the possibilities are endless!

3.10 EXPANDING YOUR SKILLS

This talk of word processing programs and spreadsheets and databases may sound like more than you want to get into, at least at first. Fine. But as I've said so often before, the more you offer, the more you get.

At the very least, you ought to consider learning how to use a word processing program and a computer. As I have already explained, the computer offers immense time savings, and the possibility of turning out letter-perfect work. Obviously, the person with the computer has a tremendous advantage over the person who is still using the old "steam" typewriter.

If you want to be able to enter a field where there is less competition and where you can charge more per hour as well (an ideal combination!), you would be very wise to learn the basics of Lotus 1-2-3. And if you want to offer a specialist service in mailing lists, where very few freelancers can compete at all, you should learn how to use a database program.

There are basically three ways to expand your skills — or, for that matter, to polish old skills. These are self-instruction, attending courses and working with a temp agency.

Self-instruction

At its simplest, this amounts to nothing more than practicing your typing. If your typing is rusty, practice (by copying the phone book, if necessary) will soon polish it again.

The next stage consists of learning from books. When you buy a computer program, it will normally have a "training" or "familiarization" section in the manual. In any case, you can learn all that you need from this, but you will usually find life very much easier if you also buy an instruction book written by someone "outside" the system. Very often, computer manuals seem to be written by computer addicts, and they are very hard for the ordinary person to read. This approach is how I learned to use both WordStar and Lotus 1-2-3. Remember that you don't necessarily have to buy the books — they are available in most libraries.

A third level involves specially-written teaching programs, which run on a computer and take you through everything in a series of graded steps. Believe it or not, there are even programs for non-typists which teach you how to touch-type! People who can already type may find them useful for increasing their speed, or for gaining familiarity with a computer.

One word of warning, though. <u>Don't</u> try to learn how to use a system before you buy it. You need to have a computer and a copy of the program so that you can work through the examples in the book. Trying to learn from a book alone is practically useless.

Colleges And Courses

Some people find it very much easier to take a course than to learn something from a book. The big advantage of a course is that if you don't understand something, you can always ask. With a book, on the other hand, you are left staring blankly at the bit you don't understand.

Almost all community colleges offer all kinds of "extension" or "extramural" or "adult education" courses, and some other groups offer them, too. If you don't know where to start looking in your community, go to your local library and ask at the information desk: they can almost always tell you where to go.

When you are looking for a course, look for one that is short and simple. Don't take a whole computer course where you must learn the theory and history of computers, and how to program them: you don't need it, and unless the teacher is unusually good, you may end up so confused that you are frightened away from computers. Instead, look for courses that last five or ten evenings and are called something like "Word Processing for Typists" or "An Introduction to Lotus 1-2-3."

Some commercial organizations offer exactly this kind of course, often as an intensive two- or three-day "seminar" or something similar. Some of these paid-for courses are very good indeed, and a very good value; others are surprisingly expensive, and could be a complete waste of money no matter how much or how little you paid. In any case, you should be able to find a community college where you can learn the same thing for twenty or thirty dollars (or even for free) instead of paying as much as $250.00 to a commercial organization.

Temp Agency Training

One option that is well worth considering is to work part-time for a temp agency for a few months. Most agencies are only too pleased to arrange courses for the people who work for them, and these are often the best courses you can find anywhere. This is because they are aimed at the real world, and at real typists, instead of being overly academic.

Don't worry about being unfair to the agency. These courses don't cost the agencies very much, and they will get their money back in the commission they earn from hiring you out. Obviously, you wouldn't want to leave as soon as you complete your first course: why should you, when you can get valuable experience *and get paid at the same time?*

3.11   EXPERIENCE

Like the often-repeated phrase about offering more and getting more, I keep coming back to little lectures on the value of experience. If you can offer a wide range of experience, you are automatically more attractive to a prospective employer. You already know about medical records? Great: a doctor isn't going to have to waste time teaching you about how to keep them. Also, if someone asks you about keeping dental records, you can say, "I've never done dental records, but I've done medical records; do you think it would be difficult for me to learn?"

Some people work best in a commercial environment; others with professional people such as lawyers or doctors; and yet others are happiest with a wide mix of different types of work. But unless you try everything, how can you find out what you like to do best, and what you can do best? Make no mistake: it is always more pleasant, and usually more profitable, to earn money doing work that you enjoy and can do well!

Don't be put off by the idea that you might need more experience in order to offer more to potential clients. Instead, look at it this way: what's six months (if that) out of your entire life, especially when you will be setting up your own business? It just might be worth your time to start out with some fresh, new experience that you can use to sell your services, and the struggle of getting better (which you definitely will) could be decreased by each day that you gain experience somewhere else!

4.0   FINDING WORK

This chapter is the main reason why you bought this book. You already know a good deal about typing; what you really want to know is how to sell your work. The news is almost all good.

I say "almost all," because ultimately, selling your work comes down to *you*. I cannot do the work for you; Broughton Hall, the publishers, cannot do the work for you; and no one else is even going to *attempt* to do the work for you. What you can learn here, though, is a selling strategy that **works**.

Once you are established, the majority of your work will come from repeat business and from word-of-mouth recommendation. Until you are established, though, you need to get your name in front of people, together with a good idea of the services you can offer. This is about how you can do this.

4.1   WHO DO YOU KNOW?

Even at the beginning, you can do a lot by word of mouth. Unless you have been out of the work force for a long time, you almost certainly know your former employers, and maybe quite a number of their suppliers and customers or clients. You know the name of the person to contact (or one of your friends can find it out for you); you know the addresses; you know the kind of work they do. This enables you to slant your advertisements and selling letters (later in this chapter) to suit their particular requirements.

Next, you have friends. Maybe some of them need things typed occasionally. I remember that, once, a man who lived across the street from me asked if I could type a letter for him. He knew that I did a lot of typing, because my desk was right next to the window, and he could often see me at work.

I told him that I wasn't in the business, but I would do it as a favor. The difficulty lay in persuading him that it was a favor: he was embarrassingly eager to pay me. If I had accepted the money (about $4 for a quarter of an hour's work), I have no doubt that he would have recommended me to his friends. He was a self-employed builder, in a small business, and more at home with bricks and mortar and lumber than with a typewriter, but he needed a professional-looking proposal to help him to get what was for him quite a big contract — maybe $1,000. He got it, too!

"Noticing" Work

This story about my neighbor is just one example of something we have all experienced — noticing things because we want to. For example, if you buy a new car, you suddenly start noticing all the other people who are driving the same car: they seem to be everywhere. The same thing will happen with typing: you will keep hearing about people who are interested in what you are doing, usually because they need some work done!

If I were looking for business, I would of course tell all my friends to spread the word, letting it be known that I was ready to type letters, proposals, or anything else for anyone who asked. I wouldn't necessarily expect my friends to need my services (though I know a few who did need a typist, and I referred them to Patsy, whom I have mentioned before), but I would expect that they would mention my name and give out my telephone number to anyone they thought might have a use for typing services.

In fact, Patsy **did** run a freelance typing bureau at home for a while, and some of her initial clients were direct referrals from me. The only reason she stopped was because her children were getting older, and spent all day at school, and she preferred to get out and meet people. It could have remained a perfectly viable business for as long as she had wanted.

Other Word-of-Mouth Advertising

Don't forget your other contacts, either. You go to the doctor, sometimes, and to a dentist. Maybe they don't need a typist (or maybe they do), but the conversation at the golf club might run something like this:

FIRST DENTIST: "I've just found out that my **** receptionist hasn't sent out any routine 'It's-time-for-your-checkup' letters for four months. There's no way she can catch up; she can barely do her job as it is — I'm going to have to let her go. I wish I had someone like your Sally ..."

SECOND DENTIST: "Just a minute — one of my clients said she was going into freelance typing. I'll get her number when I go back to the office, and call you. I don't know what she's like, but ..."

You think it doesn't happen? It does, all the time! When rich executives do it, it's called "networking," but if you're an ordinary person who is just trying to earn a living, it works in exactly the same way. People like helping other people — even people they hardly know — and our mythical dentist is helping **two** people simultaneously, his golfing friend and you. Of course, he adds the disclaimer about not knowing what you're like, but it's still an introduction.

In addition to mentioning it to your dentist, you would of course mention it to his receptionist, too. Then, next time *she* is overworked, she'll say, "Look, I don't have time to do all this — why don't I call Ms. So-and-so and see what she would charge to revise the mailing list?"

Another good idea is to make friends with your local "instant print" shops: Not only may they know people who need typing done, but they are also likely to have a good idea of who is new in town, because they will be printing their letterheads for them!

Finally, don't overlook the value of voluntary work as a means of meeting people who are willing to pay you. Typing out a list of church events for your pastor may pay nothing — but he is in a position to recommend you to all sorts of people. And if your paid work starts to take up so much time that you have to cut down on your unpaid work, well, people understand.

4.2   **THE PHONE-LETTER-PHONE APPROACH**

When approaching any organization, the best system is to break it down into three steps. First, make a telephone call to get the name and job title of the person you need to contact. In most organizations, mail which is not readily identifiable as the responsibility of a particular person is likely to end up in the "circular file."

Next, when you have the name and address of a person to write to, send an inquiry letter. There is more about inquiry letters toward the end of the chapter.

Third (if necessary), follow up your letter with another phone call to make sure that your letter arrived. Once again, there is more about this at the end of the chapter.

Now let's look at specific individuals and organizations who can (and almost certainly will) need people like *you* to work for them.

Former Employer(s)

This is particularly useful for women who have left the work force to look after their families. In all likelihood, you parted from your last employer on good terms, and you have two great advantages: first, you know the business, and second, they know you.

You can even target the specific areas in which you think they might need help: For example, "Are you still having trouble with the salesmen not writing up their orders properly? I could always type those for you ..."

A telephone call should be all you need to make this contact — and while you're asking, you might ask if your former employer knows of anyone else who might want some typing done.

4.3   OTHER LOCAL BUSINESSES

Apart from former employers, and anyone else they can put you in touch with, your next line of inquiry should be any businesses that do the same sort of thing as your previous employer.

This is also a profitable line of inquiry for anyone who is already working, and who wants to supplement his or her income by "moonlighting" — though it is worth making the point once again that *absolute discretion* is essential: gossiping about your current employer, or letting confidential commercial information be known, is a good way to make your current employer into your ex-employer, and not on good terms, either!

Here, your "sales pitch" is simple: you already know the business, and the skills you developed with your previous or present employer can be applied equally well in a similar business elsewhere. This applies even if you have moved right across the country: a small manufacturing business in Florida is likely to be run in much the same way as a small manufacturing business in Alaska, only with more open windows and fewer heavy clothes.

Once you have exhausted this line of approach, you should start looking outside your field of proven expertise, gradually widening the circle. For example, from manufacturing, you might go to distribution or wholesalers or even retailers, all in the same line of business. Then you could expand into different kinds of business, from clothing manufacturing to electronics manufacturing, from automobile distribution to artists' materials distribution.

I should emphasize that while this sounds like a lot of work, there are two important things to remember. The first is that this is pretty much a "one-time" effort: once you have built up your client list, you should go on getting repeat work with the very minimum of additional sales effort. The second is that there is a good deal of luck involved; your very first call might give you all the work you need, or you might spend all day on the phone (or writing letters) and only get a single response. Given the shortage of reliable freelance typists, and the current business climate, you should get a couple of good "bites" early on, and these will sustain you over the unresponsive parts.

4.4   NON-BUSINESS ORGANIZATIONS

There are two main groups of non-business organizations: voluntary and charitable organizations, and local (and county, state and federal) government organizations. There are also some which are a sort of hybrid between the two: Hospitals, for example, are run on a mixture of business lines and public service/local government lines.

Voluntary and Charitable Organizations

Working with these is likely to be less rewarding financially, but more rewarding in other ways. Because they rely so much on volunteerism and free work, you may have some difficulty in persuading them to pay at all; and when they do pay, they are not likely to pay very much.

On the other hand, they are more likely to be flexible in their approach — for example, they may be willing to drop work off and to pick it up, rather than expecting you to come to them

— and there is often a great "team spirit" within such organizations.

The best way to find out about these is via directories at the public library (see Chapter 7, "Resources").

Government Organizations

Above a certain level, government organizations tend to be hopelessly overstaffed; your chances of getting casual work from the Pentagon, for example, are not enormous.

At the other end of the scale, though, many city and even some county offices may be hopelessly *understaffed*: for example, parks and recreation authorities, public health clinics, libraries, and other locally administered offices.

To discover their addresses and phone numbers, look in the front of your phone directory: Local government offices are usually given in their own listing, just before the main body of names and addresses.

Hybrid Organizations

These include hospitals, as already suggested; community and other colleges (and private schools, for that matter); some theaters or arts complexes; sports complexes — the precise details will depend on your own community. The way to find out about these is through the local directories maintained at your library.

4.5   DOCTORS AND DENTISTS

The main thing that doctors and dentists need typed up is medical records and reports, so you had better be good at reading bad handwriting! This is a fairly specialized field, and you *must* buy yourself a medical dictionary, but good medical secretaries are highly valued and correspondingly highly paid.

The other thing that doctors and dentists need typed is routine medical correspondence — reminders about check-ups, results of tests, and (of course) billing.

Unless you already have some experience, this can be a difficult field to get into. There may be courses for medical secretaries at local colleges or even through temp agencies (see Chapter 3, "Expanding Your Skills"), or if you enjoy a good relationship with your own doctor, you may be able to break into it this way. Don't just think of doctors in private practice, either: remember that hospitals need typing done, as already mentioned!

Needless to say, this is a highly responsible job: badly-copied information, perhaps even the omission of a single word or the mistyping of a single dosage, could prove literally *fatal*. In the newspapers, you read from time to time about people who were accidentally given overdoses of common medications, usually by inexperienced or overtired auxiliaries who misread prescriptions. You can't stop that, but how would you feel if you had *mistyped* the prescription, and no one spotted the error? While 20 mg (milligrams) of a drug might be beneficial, 200 mg might prove fatal. This level of responsibility is one reason why medical secretaries are well paid.

4.6   LAWYERS

Lawyers are basically dealers in words, and *someone* has to get those words down on paper. Apart from legal records and client correspondence, which are much the same as medical records and correspondence, the things that lawyers need typed are contracts, wills and other agreements or deeds.

As with medical records, absolute precision is essential. For example, a lawyer can make great play of the difference between "charitable *and* benevolent" bequests in a will and "charitable *or* benevolent" bequests. In the first case, the two are read as one phrase — while in the second they are read "disjunctively," so that the money could, in theory, be applied to purposes which were benevolent but not (in the strict legal sense) charitable. Literally millions of dollars have turned on points as fine as these.

On the other hand, a great deal of legal phraseology is standardized, and whole paragraphs or even pages of a contract may be "boilerplate" — chunks of text which are as standardized and hard to alter as the sheets of steel which are used in engineering to build a heavy boiler. Many legal secretaries maintain a great deal of "boilerplate" on their word processors and read it into their standard contracts, wills, etc., as required.

Getting into legal work can be as difficult as getting into medical work, and some sort of course of study is virtually essential — but once you are in, you should always have plenty of work. Most of the lawyers in town tend to know one another, so if you are good, your reputation will rapidly spread by word of mouth.

4.7   ACCOUNTANTS — WORKING WITH NUMBERS

Accountants maintain client records, and need client correspondence, just like doctors or lawyers. There is, however, an additional possibility.

In Chapter 3, I mentioned spreadsheets and entering records. Instead of approaching small businesses directly, you might prefer to work *through* an accountant, so that he collects the shoe-boxes of records from his clients and passes them on to you for entry. The pay would probably not be all that much different, and you would be spared the effort of dealing with large numbers of individuals. Of course, he would probably charge $35 an hour and pay you $20 an hour, but what do you care? You probably couldn't charge $35 an hour anyway, unless you are a qualified accountant (in which case you can charge a lot more).

4.8   SHARED OFFICES

There are two completely different possibilities here, and both of them can be made to work.

"Work for Space"

The first is to find someone who already has an office and offer to do his (or her) typing in return for desk space. The agreement needs to be worked out fairly carefully — a maximum number of hours of their typing per week, in return for agreed times when you can use the office, with your own desk space — and you may care to have your own personal telephone line installed so that one of the lines on your desk is yours, and the other is the owner's.

One woman who did this found that by working in an attorney's office, she could earn $600 a week with literally *no* expenses (she didn't have her own line). She had desk space, a good business address, a telephone, access to a fax and photocopier, and a high level of "instant credibility." All she had to do was answer his phones — if he wanted typing, he paid her for it! He, in return, had a receptionist who cost him virtually nothing. It was a classic "win-win" situation.

Co-op Offices

These are still sufficiently unusual that they require a bit of explanation. They are normally older office buildings which have been refurbished and specially set up for rental as small units. The unit may be anything from a suite of offices, through a single small office, to a desk in a shared office.

They attract all kinds of people. In one that a friend of mine used to use, there were computer consultants, commercial artists, architects, an accountant, an import-export business, and even a restaurant on the ground floor!

The big attraction of these places is that because many of the facilities are shared, the cost of setting up an office is much less than if you had to pay for everything yourself. For example, there is usually a receptionist/switchboard operator whose salary is part of the rent; a shared photocopier (with a "key card" for apportioning actual copy cost); a fax; a coffee machine — AND NO TYPIST!

This gives you two options. One is to take a desk at the shared office, and work as a freelance typing pool, and the other is to continue to work at home, but to work for everyone else in the shared office. You can either walk around the office, introducing yourself personally and collecting and returning work, or work through the receptionist/switchboard operator, usually in return for a ten percent cut to him or her. Giving away ten percent of your income may stick in your craw a bit, but when you consider how much work he or she can give you, why worry?

4.9   BUSINESS FAIRS

In any city of any size, there are all kinds of business and other fairs, all through the year. The bigger the city, the more the fairs, but *any* city of more than 50,000 inhabitants should have at least a half a dozen a year.

Your local Chamber of Commerce (more about them later, as well as in Chapter 7) can usually let you have a list of these fairs, and if you go to them in person, you may be able to pick up a surprising amount of business. The people on the stands are there to sell, rather than to buy; but equally, if you are offering a service they need, they are buying!

The great advantage of visiting these fairs is that you meet people face-to-face. For small businesses, you will meet the principals: for bigger businesses, you will meet people who can give you the names you need to contact.

Writers' Conferences

These are like business fairs for writers; they gather to talk shop, listen to lectures, meet agents and generally have a good time. Put an ad in the program for one of these, or even go along to a local one, and you may be surprised at how much work you can pick up! (A comprehensive listing of writers' conferences is included in Broughton Hall's publication entitled *Earn Money Reading Books*.) I'll come back to manuscript typing shortly.

4.10 OTHER POSSIBILITIES

There are many, many other possibilities, and it is only possible to list a few of the more important ones here.

Advertising Agencies

Advertising agencies normally work on a "boom or bust" basis. In the "boom" times, they *always* need more help. It may well be worth approaching advertising agencies as much as twenty or thirty miles away, letting them know that you can offer a fast and reliable service when they have a "screamer." Of course, you can charge handsomely for this sort of work!

Authors

Fewer and fewer authors are putting their manuscripts out for typing, as more and more of them buy word processors and do all the work themselves.

Even so, there are still some authors who feel that a professionally typed manuscript adds a certain something to their presentation. There are others who cannot work straight into a keyboard, and who prefer to use old-fashioned methods of cut-and-paste, marginal notes, additions and so forth; they then hand you the stack of grubby bits of paper, which you are supposed to turn into a sparkling manuscript!

Few authors have much money, and many will buy on price alone, so before you accept a job, always inquire carefully what sort of state the manuscript is in. If it is a genuinely handwritten manuscript, or if it is a mass of cut-and-paste, you are looking at a lot more work than if you are just retyping a novel which has already been (somewhat amateurishly) typed on an old manual typewriter.

Churches

Few ministers preach from long, fully-typed sermons any more — working from more or less extensive notes is the order of the day — but churches still need newsletters; calendars of forthcoming events; orders of service; instructional material for catechism classes or Sunday School; and various other sorts of typing.

They will not necessarily pay well, and they may not even pay at all, but they offer an excellent way of becoming known in the parish!

Insurance Brokers

For preparing complex quotes, and for regular reminder letters to their clients, many insurance brokers could do with a freelance typist.

Photographers

Many freelance photographers need someone to type their letters, chase their clients, catalog their pictures, and a great deal more. They are more likely to be interested in someone who can offer a full range of secretarial services than in a copy-typist.

Public Relations Companies

These operate rather like advertising agencies (see above), on a "boom or bust" basis, and may well have the same kind of need for typists to work on "screamers."

Production Companies

Although Hollywood might seem like the only place for script and similar typing, you might be surprised at how many small film, video and animation studios are spread all over the country. Look in the Yellow Pages under "Film Producers" and "Video Services."

Realtors

Ever wonder who types up those descriptions of houses that realtors hand out all the time? *Someone* has to do it!

Restaurateurs

You'll never get rich typing menus, but it's a service that a lot of restaurants need — and if they change their menu every few days, as is usual with good restaurants, it's steady work. They can even phone the list of menu choices to you; if you can turn up the next day with (say) two dozen photocopies and an original, they will be well pleased.

Do be careful, though, to spell things correctly — get a dictionary if need be. Many restaurants use French names, and they don't even spell things correctly themselves. For example, had you ever realized that the word is <u>restaurateur</u> and not <u>restauranteur</u>?

Resume Writing

Professional resume writing can be a *very* lucrative field, especially if you help compose the resume as well as typing it and having it printed. You will need to advertise in the business press if you want to pick up resume work, but I have heard of professional resume writers who charge up to $300 *per resume*. There is more about resume writing in the next chapter.

Scanner Typing

Some businesses use "scanners" which can read typewritten text straight into a computer. The text must, however, be in a very definite form: the typeface, the spacing, and the width of the margins are all rigorously defined. For obvious reasons, they need copy-typists!

Theaters

Theaters need programs and (sometimes) scripts typed. Someone has to do it!

Veterinarians

Everyone thinks of doctors and dentists when you say "medical records" — but animals have medical records, too!

4.11 ADVERTISING

For most small businesses, continuous advertising in the general media (newspapers, magazines, etc.) is an expensive waste of time. Just think about how you read a newspaper. Do you even notice the advertisements? Could you name a single advertisement that appeared in yesterday's newspaper?

No: you need a different advertising strategy. If you are going to pay for your advertising, you had better *target* it carefully so that it is seen by people who might need typing and related services. You also need to get advertisements where they are **seen**, instead of being lost in a morass of other information. And thirdly, you need to *be specific* about what you offer.

"Targeted" Advertising

An example of "targeted" advertising might be in a magazine aimed at writers if you offer manuscript typing, or more generally, in a local Chamber of Commerce publication that is seen by many local businessmen. If you actually *join* the Chamber of Commerce (Chapter 7), they will very probably mention you in the newsletter for nothing — which is very cheap advertising indeed!

Again, the "classified" section of a business magazine might be the best place to advertise a resume service. I'm not talking about *Forbes Magazine* or something similar: I'm talking about the kind of specialized magazines that are sent out to professional engineers, or the catering industry, or whatever — advertising in these can be surprisingly cheap!

The Yellow Pages are a sort of in-between listing: people only read them when they need a service. Are they going to need *your* service? I suggest that the answer is "Yes," *if* you word your advertisement clearly. Use the "Secretarial Service" entry, and make your listing as comprehensive as possible, as described below.

What's in a Name?

You may decide to call yourself ANNE SMITH TYPING SERVICE (which could be a one-woman operation or a huge bureau), or you could make a virtue of the fact that you are on your own: There are plenty of people who distrust big organizations, and who would prefer to deal with the same recognizable individual each time they call, rather than with an ever-changing panorama of receptionists and temporary typists. Instead of being worth *less* to these people than a big agency, you are worth *more*.

You may also decide to use a name which gives an idea of your specialty, such as MEDI-TYPE, or SCRIPTS UNLIMITED, or LEGAL EAGLE TYPING, but bear in mind that this can also **limit** the range of work that people think of offering to you.

Business Cards

Of course, you will have business cards printed, and hand them out as widely as possible. This not only looks professional, it also means that people have a convenient written record of your name and address. Don't try to make the business card into a circus poster. Something like this should be plenty:

```
┌─────────────────────────────────────────────┐
│                                               │
│               ANNE SMITH                      │
│                                               │
│        Typing and Secretarial Services        │
│                                               │
│                                               │
│   123 High Street                             │
│   Anytown, AS  94076         Tel. (213) 555-2121 │
│                                               │
└─────────────────────────────────────────────┘
```

Bulletin Board Advertising

The real "sleeper," the means of advertising that brings people in and keeps right on bringing them in, is likely to be bulletin-board advertising. This is usually free (though you may need to put up a new advertisement every week or every month), and if it's in a place where people read the bulletin boards, you can generate a truly surprising amount of work.

For example, students need theses and term papers typed, so why not put up a notice on a college bulletin board? Clear it with the college authorities first, of course, but they are unlikely to withhold permission. Again, many camera stores have a bulletin board for clubs, people buying and selling cameras, and so forth. Plenty of freelance photographers need freelance secretarial services, and they may well copy down your name and phone number (generally safer than giving an address).

The list of possibilities for this kind of direct, pinned-to-the-wall advertising is enormous: libraries, sports clubs, churches — the list goes on forever. Remember, too, that people are multi-dimensional. Merely because someone sees your name on a church bulletin board or a sports club notice board, it does not necessarily mean that he (or she) will want you to do specifically religious or sporting work. The person who sees that notice might be a lawyer, or a builder, or a realtor, or almost anyone.

Furthermore, people like to work with people who have the same interests as them. If you attend the same church, or you or your spouse goes to a particular sports club, it means that you have a better chance than a complete stranger.

Yes, but what do you *DO?*

It is hard to over-emphasize the importance of being as specific as possible about what you do. In this respect, your "postcards" are completely different from your business cards. For example, ANNE SMITH — TYPIST, Telephone (213) 555-2121 may be clear and concise, but it doesn't get people's *immediate* attention. They don't want a generic typist; they want someone who can type *their* work. A much better advertisement (which would still fit on a 3x5 index card that could be pinned anywhere) might read:

```
            TYPING BY ANNE SMITH


    Specializing in letters, medical and legal
records, term papers and theses. Also property
descriptions for realtors; business proposals;
resumes; newsletters; and anything else you want
typed. North Los Angeles area. Call (213)
555-2121.
```

This brings us back to the point I have made repeatedly: if you offer more, you can earn more. Imagine being able to write:

```
              TYPING BY ANNE SMITH

    Specializing in letters, medical and legal
records, term papers and theses. Also property
descriptions for realtors; business proposals;
resumes; newsletters; and anything else you want
typed.

    I can also offer statistical typing; filing;
record-keeping; and entering invoices (receiv-
able and payable) on a Lotus 1-2-3 spreadsheet.
Make life easier next April 15!

    South Los Angeles area. Call (213) 555-2121.
```

See what I mean?

4.12 ADVERTISING YOURSELF BY MAIL

If you are advertising your skills as someone who is able to turn out polished letters and resumes, it seems reasonable that you should be able to do a good job of writing a selling letter. Even if you have no literary skills whatsoever and are a copy-typist pure and simple, you should be able to find a friend who will help you put together a short, crisp selling letter. Type it up on good-quality headed paper, put it in a good-quality envelope, and send it to people.

Because this is a sample of your work, it *must* be an original typed letter (not printed), it *must* be on the best paper you can possibly afford, and it *must* be absolutely flawless in all senses. This means technically (no white-out, no dog-ears); grammatically (including spelling and punctuation); and stylistically (follow the conventions for layout on page 86).

Use a Name

Always address your letters to a specific person if you can get their name. This greatly reduces the chance of your letter being discarded immediately as "junk mail." Opinions are divided about whether you should write "Ms. Jones" or "Jane Jones" (assuming you don't know whether she is Mrs. or Miss). "Ms. Jones" appears to be more popular.

To get someone's name, just call the switchboard, or use a directory as described in Chapter 7. Even if you have a name from a directory, call the switchboard anyway; the person whose name you have may have left, and you can ask who has taken over their responsibilities. If in doubt, ask for the name of the office manager — and if they say they don't have an office manager, just explain briefly, saying something like:

"My name is Anne Smith, and I'm launching a typing service. I wanted to send a letter to whomever it is in your company that might need typing done. I realize you might not need it now, but I thought it would be useful for both of us if you had it on file."

I've never had anyone refuse to give me a name when I've asked like this. I might never get an answer to the letter, but at least I know it's gone to the right place!

Be Brief

If they like the look and feel of the letter, they'll call back. If they don't, they won't — and they won't bother to read a super-long letter, either, even if you took time to type it flawlessly.

SAMPLE LETTER
(using headed paper)

**Anne Smith, 44 High Street, Anytown, AN 123456
Tel. (213) 555-1212**

June 12, 1999

Ms. Jane Jones,
Office Manager
The Widget Corporation
Widget House
101 Broadway
Anytown, AN 1234567

Dear Jane Jones:

A crisp, well-typed letter is an invaluable ambassador for your company -- and we all know the value of getting a letter out on time! For those times when your secretarial department is overloaded, or when vacations and sickness mean that you are understaffed, I can offer a fast, reliable typing service which meets the high standards you expect.

In addition to letters, I also type company reports, statistical lists, mailing lists, records, and so forth. I also type resumes, though I hope there is no one in your organization who is in need of one of these!

If you are interested, or if you would just like to call and get acquainted in case we can work together later, why not call me at the above number? I am normally there in the mornings, though in the afternoons you may get my answering machine because I am out picking up and dropping off work and going to the post office.

Yours sincerely,

Anne Smith

4.13   ADVERTISING YOURSELF ON THE TELEPHONE

The response from a direct mail marketing campaign is rarely spectacular: if you get replies from one-tenth of the people you wrote to, you are doing well.

Likewise, "cold calling" on the telephone is not something that most people relish — and that applies to both making the calls and to receiving them.

If, however, you combine the two, and follow up your letter a week later with a phone call, you can get a very much higher response rate than either would produce on its own.

This also gives you twice the chance of finding the right person. Presumably, you will have called the company switchboard already to find out the name of the person you are writing to; but if you got their name from someone else, and you are connected to someone completely different, you have an additional chance to make your pitch. So what do you have to talk about?

To begin with, the mere fact that you are calling means that you are reinforcing the message that there's someone new out there, someone who is ready and willing to work, someone who is not afraid to hustle a bit. *This is important:* if your clients see you as a "shrinking violet," they will often take advantage of you by asking for impossible deadlines, delaying payment, beating down the price, giving you more work than you contracted for, and so forth. They don't want out-and-out hardball, but they do want someone they can respect.

Secondly, you have something to talk about. Have they received the letter? If they have, you tell them that you're just following it up to see if they might be able to use you some time in the future. If they haven't, you deliver basically the same message that is in the letter. In some ways, you are almost better off if they have not read your letter: people are generally apologetic if they haven't received a letter, as if it were their fault. You can promise to send a follow-up (and make sure you do!), and you can be sure that it will be read.

Be Prepared

You will have to have the answers ready to a few hard questions. The first and hardest is likely to be, "What do you charge?" You had better have done your homework on this, as described on page 31.

You will probably be asked where you are; what sort of work you have handled in the past; whether you can pick up and deliver work (though the sample letter already answers this one); and what sort of turn-around time you have. If you are asked your typing speed, you have the option of either telling them truth, or exaggerating slightly: after all, they are only going to see the finished work, and if it takes you two hours to do a one-hour job because you can only type 30 wpm instead of 60 wpm, that is your problem rather than theirs. If you actually charge an hourly rate but are quite a slow typist, it's obvious you will need to make adjustments until you improve your speed.

If you are asked who your other clients are, you can answer truthfully, answer in general terms, or simply say that you regard that as confidential information, and that you would of course respect their privacy as you respect that of your other clients. This is particularly useful if you don't actually *have* any other clients yet!

You may also be asked what sort of computer system you use. If you can answer that you have an IBM-compatible computer with both 5¼" and 3½" disk drives, your credibility goes up magically: the chances are that you can swap disks with them, which makes everything much easier for everyone. But if you are still soldiering along with a typewriter, don't be afraid to make the selling point of that, too: "Oh, just an old IBM Selectric — I've been using it so long that I can't bear to convert to a computer." You may get a certain sympathy vote here!

Do not neglect the possibility of "semi-cold" calling, either. If a friend has told you about someone they know who might need a typist, look them up in the phone book and call them. The reason for looking the number up is because if your friend has given you the unlisted number of **his** friend, their friendship may be somewhat strained as a result! Make it clear that you got the number from the phone book, for this very reason. If it's an unlisted number, ask your friend to contact the other person and ask if it's okay for you to call.

5.0   <u>TYPES OF WORK</u>

In the previous chapter, I said a good deal about the different kinds of work that were required by different types of people; I have arranged them in alphabetical order.

<u>Addressing and "Stuffing" Envelopes</u>

This is something you can do with just a typewriter and a stack of envelopes and letters or catalogs (supplied by the client!). It doesn't pay very well — it's at the bottom end of the skill range, and therefore at the bottom end of the price range too — but it's easy, and it's better than no work!

<u>Business and Other Proposals</u>

In order to get business, many professional people, manufacturers, and others have to submit a proposal which tells the prospective client what they can expect for their money.

Because these proposals are *extremely* important, and may have taken several weeks (or even months) of work just to prepare, presentation is of the utmost importance. They are normally beautifully typed, on the finest-quality paper.

The cover sheet normally contains *only* the name of the project (or whatever the proposal is), the name of the person or firm preparing the proposal, and the name of the person for whom it is prepared. The paper should be so heavy that there is no chance of type "reading through" from the page beneath. Subsequent pages are typed double-spaced with wide margins and plenty of "working space" around the text. This is not just to look good: it is so the client can write notes in the margins.

You need to follow your clients' directions closely, but do not be afraid to make your own suggestions for making a proposal look better — for example, the use of centering, boldface, and overall layout of text.

Church Programs

A church program normally lists the order of the service first (or, in the case of a folded program, on the left) while below or on the right there are announcements of forthcoming events, programs, etc. With some folded programs, the back page may carry paid advertising.

Correspondence

The technical requirements for correspondence are no longer as rigid as they used to be. For example, when I was a child, I was always taught that different types of letters were begun and ended in different ways. The three traditional types were:

BEGINNING	END
Dear Sir (or Dear Madam)	Yours faithfully
Dear Mr. Smith (or Mrs. Jones)	Yours sincerely
Dear John (or Jane)	Yours truly

While individual clients may have their own specific requirements (which you should always follow if they tell you), the typical layout for a business letter is shown in Example 1. Your address (or the address of the company or person for whom you are typing, if they don't have their own printed letterhead) goes on the upper right; this is followed two lines down by the date; then five lines down and on the left is the "inside address" (person to whom the letter is going); and two more lines down is the "greeting".

EXAMPLE 1

The XYZ Company
XYZ House, Anywhere Road
Anytown, AS 123456

February 30, 1999

Mr. John Smith
President, J. Smith & Co.
123 Broadway, Suite 1
Anytown, AS 123457

Dear Mr. Smith,

Thank you for your payment of $1,234.56 in respect of...

(THE REST OF THE LETTER IS HERE)

Yours sincerely,

Mary Jones,
Chief Executive Officer

There are many possible variations. For example, the way in which you lay out the address is governed by what looks best: if the company in the example had no suite number, you might choose to write:

94

Mr. John Smith
President
J. Smith & Co.
Anytown, AS 123457

Also, any "reference" remarks normally go just under the inside address, as follows:

EXAMPLE 2

The XYZ Company
XYZ House, Anywhere Road
Anytown, AS 123456

February 30, 1999

Mr. John Smith
President, J. Smith & Co.
123 Broadway, Suite 1
Anytown, AS 123457

Your reference: JS/wc/21-1
Our reference: A/C No. ABC 12345

Dear Mr. Smith,

    Thank you for payment of $1,234.56 in respect of...

        (THE REST OF THE LETTER IS HERE)

Yours sincerely,

Mary Jones,
Chief Executive Officer

Formal Greetings

The formal greeting can vary widely: although "Dear Mr. Smith" is traditional, "Dear John Smith" is becoming more popular, and if Mary Jones knows John Smith quite well, she might just write "Dear John." Ask what the client wants.

Formal greetings for women are a nightmare for those who love old-fashioned etiquette: "Dear Mrs.," "Dear Miss," and "Dear Ms." are all used, along with "Dear Mary Jones" and of course "Dear Mary." Ask the client for guidance. I normally use Ms., even though I know there are some people who do not like it.

Ending the Letter

All kinds of "sign-offs" are used, such as "Sincerely" or "With best regards" or (as I used to get from one Scots publisher) "Yours Aye." Use these only if your client specifically instructs you to do so — or if in doubt, ASK.

If you are signing *for* someone (as your client might ask you to do on a routine letter like this), you sign your name and then type or hand-write "pp" or "p.p." in front of the typed signature — in our example, Mary Jones. This stands for *pro parte,* which is Latin for "on behalf of."

Remember, if you need a refresher course on how to lay out different types of business correspondence, there are almost certainly several books in your local library on how to do this. You could even go and buy one in a local bookstore.

Data Entry

With the increasing use of IBM-compatible computers, you **may** be able to get this modern equivalent of copy-typing. As more and more people transfer from manual files to computers, there is a constant demand for "data entry." If your machine can handle your client's software, you can do this at home.

What you are paid to do is to transfer information from an old, typed or hand-written format to a computer disk. This may be "straight" copy-typing, or it may involve filling in "fields." For example, medical records might begin with:

NAME: LAST_____ FIRST_____ MIDDLE/INIT_____

STREET ADDRESS _____

CITY_____ STATE _____ ZIP _____

TELEPH: H ME_____ W RK_____

DATE F BIRTH:_____

The hand-written record tells you that Dolores Hayes was born on January 1, 1950 and lives at 44 Humbert Lane, Nabokov, IL 1234; her home phone number is (555) 123-3456.

You therefore key in HAYES, and hit the return (or "enter" key). The screen pointer (cursor) moves to FIRST, and you key in DOLORES and hit "enter" and the cursor moves to ADDRESS: STREET. You key in 44 HUMBERT LANE, "enter," then NABOKOV, then "enter" and so forth.

It's not exciting work, but it's very necessary, and if you have the equipment for it and can do it, it pays better than ordinary copy-typing. It does require that you be very accurate, because few people want to proofread long lists of names and addresses, but they would certainly be embarrassed if their mailings had misspelled names or other inaccurate information; not to mention the expense of remailing items which are returned for incorrect addresses. In the nature of things, it tends to be "one-time" work (people only transfer to computers once, after all), but, if you did a good job entering data, you may also be able to get work updating existing records, or entering regularly-received data like sales orders, etc.

Mailing Lists

At one time you could make money by taking a company's card-file of customers and typing it into a mailing list. Today, a computer is essential if you are to keep the mailing list up-to-date.

On the bright side, if you do have a company's mailing list on disk, you may well be able to get a lot of routine work out of them — everything from advertising circulars to Christmas cards. What's more, with a good word-processing program, you can even "merge print" a standard letter with the whole mailing list. That way, each letter is personally addressed to Mr. Smith, or Ms. Jones, or Davy Jones, Esq., or whomever.

You can also create mailing lists by using standard directories, as described in Chapter 7. For example, you could extract all local law firms from the Martindale-Hubbard Directory — a useful mailing list for (say) a legal typing service, such as your own.

As mentioned in Chapter 3, you can set up really clever mailing lists on a computer, using a database system. This is normally only worthwhile for a really big organization: for example, a large department store. Then, they might welcome the ability to target "all married female customers under 35 on the affluent (west) side of town," to tell them about a new line of children's clothes.

Mailing Lists as A Business

In fact, mailing lists are regularly bought and sold. Suppose a company is selling electronic goods by mail: they would love to get their hands on a list of everyone in your city who has bought electronic goods from a local store in the last eighteen months. Large fortunes have been built on selling mailing lists.

Manuscripts

As already mentioned, the big trouble with typing authors' manuscripts is that few authors have much money. It does not, therefore, pay well.

Even so, it can be very entertaining and interesting work — imagine seeing a best-seller before anyone else, even the publisher! — and all authors know that a well-presented manuscript makes a better impression than a dog-eared one. Leave wide margins; double-space the work; give an extra space between paragraphs; indent paragraphs five spaces; and ask the author whether they want anything more than plain numbering on the manuscript. This last is more important than you might think.

My manuscripts are just numbered at the bottom of the page, in the middle (1...2...3...4 etc.), but some writers believe that each new page should have their name and an abbreviation of title (or the whole title, if it is short) in the top right-hand corner, together with the page number. Then, at the bottom of the page, they may want to type "-MORE-." If you were typing a book called "Red Alert" for a man called John Bloggins, the second page might therefore look like this:

Bloggins/Red Alert 2

as the cold rain began to fall. He hunched his shoulders despondently, turning up his collar for a little extra protection, but a rivulet of water soon began to trickle down the back of his neck.

From the cafe across the road, Annette watched him. Poor fool! Why did he always have to make life difficult for himself? She wondered...
[Several paragraphs omitted here]

The rain eased a little, but it didn't make much difference. He was soaked through anyway. All I need now, he thought, is for

-MORE-

Movie Scripts

Movie scripts — and typewritten play-scripts, for that matter — *don't* look like the plays you may have read at school. There's much more blank paper, and sometimes movie scripts are typed for the principal characters which contain *only* their lines, plus their cues. This makes it easier to learn the lines; the actor or actress then studies the rest of the play (or movie, or whatever) using full script.

The technical requirements are normally tightly defined, but fairly few in number. There are various different conventions, and the commissioning studio will tell you what they are, but a fairly typical layout involves centering the characters' names and distinguishing between stage directions and dialogue by using brackets and by using wider margins for the dialogue. The names of the characters are normally in capitals in the stage directions, as shown.

SCOTT

And what do you think you're doing?

(Scott walks across the room toward DEIRDRE, who

shrinks away from him)

ARTHUR

Steady on, old man! It wasn't her fault, you know. In fact...

Well, if you want the truth...

If you are using a printer which allows you to switch between italics and normal (Roman) type, such as a laser printer or some LQ dot-matrix printers, you may put the stage directions in italics.

Newsletters

This is where the owner of a laser printer can <u>really</u> score, because of the superb typeset quality of the finished product. Even if you don't have access to a laser printer (and remember what was said earlier about going to a copy-shop to rent one), you can still turn out a highly professional-looking newsletter: you can even get by with a plain old electric typewriter, because white-outs and other corrections don't show when the newsletter is reproduced!

Record-keeping

Technical requirements for medical, legal and other records vary so widely that it is impossible to give general advice — except, perhaps, for two things. One is to type up one sample record, following the format you have been given, and submit that to check that everything is correct, before you type any more! The other is that if you have *any* questions about *anything*, check the answers before you go any further. Clients will develop great respect for you if you ask questions about things that you don't understand or that don't look right; it shows that you are paying attention to what you are doing, and it can also eliminate costly or embarrassing mistakes.

Resumes

Most people want one of two things when looking for a typist to prepare their resume, either (1) someone to simply format and type the information they already have — in other words, make their existing information *look good* — or (2) someone to actually *compose* their resume for them, based on information given during an interview or on many scraps of paper they hand you with all kinds of information on it! The "knack" for composing resumes is not something that everyone has, so if you don't feel comfortable taking the responsibility for telling someone else's history, *don't* advertise that you can do it! You will be respected for doing whatever work you do well, but resumes are VERY personal to people, so they *must* be well written. If you are especially interested in learning to compose resumes, there are all kinds of books at the library that can help you; not only is it a lucrative field, but it's very interesting and satisfying as well ... you learn all about the people you help, and most are extremely grateful for your expertise!

The normal format for a modern resume is "reverse chronological" — in other words, it begins with the present and works backwards.

After giving the person's name (often in bold type), you give the address and phone number. If appropriate, you may also include date of birth and other personal information — for example, a dancer might want it to be known that she was 22 years old, 5 feet, 6 inches tall and 36-24-35. The age and dimensions of a potential Chief Executive Officer might be more closely guarded secrets.

Next comes education, followed by previous experience. Anything more than a one-page resume is likely to be ignored by many companies as long-winded and not "punchy enough." According to one survey, the average time spent "reading" (more like "glancing at") a typical unsolicited resume is 5 seconds! On the other hand, if you are preparing a resume for an executive or other high-ranking professional, be sure you do NOT attempt to cram two pages worth of information onto one page; all the information is necessary (because of their level of expertise), and it must be typed to *look professional.*

There are also many books available (either in bookshops or in your library) which deal *specifically* with how to write resumes, and if you want to get into the resume-writing business in a big way, you ought to read at least one of them. For a basic resume, though, the layout might look like this (note the use of spacing and bold type):

TOM JONES
345 Delilah Street, Fielding, Iowa 123456
Telephone (555) 123-4567 Fax (555) 123-4568

EDUCATION
M.A. (Musicology), University of Utrecht, 1969.
B.A. (Liberal Arts), Miami University, Oxford, OH 1966.
Eton College, 1952-1958.

EXPERIENCE
Director, Fielding City Opera, 1984-present.
Responsibilities include Administration and Fund-
raising, Artistic Development, Preparation of Annual
Budget. Working with various volunteer fund-raising
groups, Grant Writing, supervision of staff of 30.

Deputy Director, Fielding Sinfonietta 1981-1984.
Responsibilities included booking venues, contracts,
fund-raising. Played French Horn occasionally in
Sinfonietta; lectured at Fielding Community College
(part time).

**Teacher of Music and Musicology, Fielding Junior High
School**, 1973-1981. Additional responsibilities
including coaching school boxing and chess teams.

U.S. Army, 1969-1973. Mostly stationed in Germany.

This <u>very</u> brief and "punchy" resume has the advantage that the present job is in the psychological "hot spot," about a third of the way down, where it is likeliest to be noticed.

Theater Programs

Theater programs can range from a single 8½"x11" page to a large booklet. Generally, anything more than a single-folded 8½"x11" program will contain a great deal of advertising.

The standard features in a play program are as follows:

Title and author. The positioning and size of this may be a part of the contract under which the play is licensed, and must be carefully checked. There may also be other contractual requirements, such as the name of the leaseholding company; the name of the first producer; or other information. If you are aware of this, the theater company will have all the more respect for you — and remember, these people may be in a position to give you other work.

Cast of Characters. The order of these is sometimes a matter of dispute, as most actors and actresses have a very high opinion of themselves. Also, check the spelling of the players' names very carefully!

Producer and director, often with biographies. This information may appear before or after the cast of characters.

Other credits: choreography, music, technical and lighting, wardrobe master/mistress, loan of props, etc.

Order of scenes (as in "Scene One, Act One — The Castle of King Verence, Friday Afternoon," or "Scene One, Act Two — The Same, Later").

Speeches and Sermons

With these, ease of legibility is the important thing. Doubles or even triple spacing is the rule, and the margins either side are wide: the text may be as little as 50 characters between margins.

For the same reasons, pica (10-pitch) is more usual than elite (12-pitch).

Spreadsheets

To print out a full-size spreadsheet, you may well need a wide-carriage (132-column) printer. In order to keep the size of the spreadsheet within bounds, use a small typeface (elite rather than pica) and, if you have the option, set your printer at 15 characters per inch rather than 10 or 12.

Theses and Term Papers

These probably have the most stringent technical requirements of all kinds of typing. For some reason, many professors seem to think that they can grade their students' papers on how closely they stick to the college's rules concerning presentation, and many students lose more grade points for sloppy presentation than they do for sloppy research or poor content!

What is worse, requirements vary from college to college. Typical specifications include:

- Overall character width — typically 55, 60 or 65 characters between margins.

- Requiring two spaces after a period instead of one, or one instead of two.

- Width of left, right, upper and lower margins.

- Single spacing instead of double spacing, although double spacing is much more usual.

- Positioning of numbering on the page.

- Positioning of footnotes, whether at the foot of the page or at the end of the text.

- Headings — capitals, underlining, etc.

- Cover page format.

- Use of abbreviations.

- Use of "APA" style for citing quoted material (explained in publications mentioned in the next paragraph).

Virtually *all* colleges and universities either have their own style book or they will tell the students which to get and use. You can easily get this information from the campus bookstore or the graduate school, then purchase the guides yourself. They are very inexpensive, and it's likely you won't have more than two or three colleges and/or universities in your immediate area; if you know how to do these documents, many grateful students will probably find their way to your door!

So much for types of work, how to find them and how to deal with them. What we're going to look at next is a much more enjoyable subject to dream about — How to Cope with Success.

6.0 COPING WITH SUCCESS

At the end of Chapter 1, I advised you to start out modestly, and to work at home. But as you earn more and more money from typing at home, you are going to have to decide how you want to go on. Do you want to continue in the same way, or are you going to spend a bit more money on more and better equipment, and make this into a "real" business?

Quite honestly, I don't see the point of renting an office outside the home, if you can possibly continue to work at home. There are a few exceptions, such as working in the type of co-op office mentioned in Chapter 4, but mostly, you're laying out a lot of money for no real advantages — unless you're *very* pressed for space, and even then, an addition to the house might pay for itself in a couple of years. On the other hand, if your business has grown to the point where you no longer can afford the time to pick up and deliver all jobs, how accessible is your home to the majority of your clients?

As you become more of a "real" business (if you even *want* to), there are various questions you'll need to answer; and these are dealt with, as briefly as possible, in this chapter. After all, by the time you have to start worrying about many of these questions, you'll be a pretty seasoned businessman or businesswoman, and there will probably be a number of tips *you* could give *me*!

Broadly, there are five areas you need to deal with. One is the office telephone; the second is office furniture; the third is additional office equipment such as a fax (facsimile) machine; the fourth is concerned with legal and technical matters; and the fifth is what to do when you have more work than you can handle. It can happen, believe me, and if you follow the advice given in this book and work hard at your own business, it very likely *will* happen.

6.1 OFFICE TELEPHONE

An additional office telephone is essential if you share a house —
you don't want someone else answering your business calls — and
desirable even if you live alone or with your family. At the very least, you
must have an extension beside your desk, so that you can be reached
easily.

On the other hand, don't worry about the phone being
accidentally answered by your four-year-old daughter. Some people get
really uptight about their clients finding out that they are a one-woman
show working from home — but why? If you are honest with your
clients, and if the work comes in clean and on time, they don't care
where you work.

6.2 ANSWERING MACHINE

An answering machine is a virtual necessity, whether you have an
office line or a home line. The message on mine says briefly that neither
my wife nor I is at home at the moment, but that if the caller would like
to leave a message, we'll get back to them. I reckon that the answering
machine has earned me thousands: if people couldn't leave a message
on my machine, they'd just try the next writer on their list. Likewise, if
you don't have a message on *your* answering machine, they'll call the
next typist on their list.

6.3 OFFICE FURNITURE

I have earned many thousands of dollars working at a table which
the previous owner of my house left behind when he moved, with
additional desk area provided by a table I bought in a second-hand shop
for $18. My chair was another $7 at a thrift shop, supplemented by a
cushion inherited from my grandmother. Of my two filing cabinets, one
cost me $8 at a going-out-of-business sale, and the other was $30 at
auction. These prices were all about ten years ago, but they are hardly
crippling if you triple them!

In other words, you don't have to go to expensive office-equipment suppliers to buy your furniture. Thrift shops, auction, and even friends' discards can provide all you need!

Chairs

The main requirements here are solidity and comfort. When I left England, I left my $7 chair behind, and spent $59.95 (in 1987) on a new office chair. It was a waste of money! I should either have spent $15-$20 on a chair at a thrift shop, or $180 on the chair I really wanted. The cheap typing chair had to be repaired after eighteen months, and I'll be lucky if it lasts five years. As the old saying goes, "quality doesn't cost — it pays."

Desks

Again, I left my old tables behind, but I think my new ones are an improvement — artists' drafting tables, adjustable for height. Extra working area is provided by a sheet of heavy, high-quality plywood spread on the tops of my filing cabinets!

Filing Cabinets

These are more useful than you might think, but you don't need many of them: one three-or-four-drawer cabinet may well be enough, and two will be plenty. If you buy them new, you may be able to find them for as little as $100 each: in thrift stores or at auction, $20 each is more like it!

6.4   OTHER OFFICE EQUIPMENT

The three main pieces of office equipment that you should consider (after your computer) are a "feature" phone; a fax machine; and a photocopier. A modem — an electronic device for exchanging information between computers — is worth considering for some applications.

"Feature" Phones

These are phones with extras such as memory/auto-dialing and other features such as on-hook dialing and hands-free speakerphone operation. They will save you a good deal of time, and are surprisingly cheap — under $100. Or, of course, many faxes have phones with these features built in.

Facsimile Machines (Faxes)

Everyone I know who has a fax machine is utterly convinced that it has paid for itself many times over. The ability to communicate with people instantaneously, world-wide, without playing "telephone tag" (You get back to me — I'll get back to you — You get back to me...) is tremendous. It is also excellent for getting a rush letter or signed contract to someone else with a fax — they get it as fast as a phone call instead of being at the mercy of the Postal Service or the expense of Federal Express.

In your line of business, the fax has two advantages. One is that you can communicate swiftly and accurately with those of your clients who have fax machines of their own. It gives you the ability to fax short drafts to your clients at their home or place of business, and they can return the revised draft the same way, saving you or them from unnecessary deliveries/pickups. The second is that you can communicate swiftly and accurately <u>on behalf of</u> your clients who do <u>not</u> have fax machines of their own.

In any modern business, giving a fax number is very good indeed for looking professional, and your clients may well welcome being able to use your machine to send or receive faxes. When you consider that $1 per sheet is the **minimum** normally charged for sending or receiving faxes, and that fees as high as $3.50 per sheet are not unknown, you can see how a fax could pay for itself very quickly indeed. On outgoing calls, you are paying only the cost of the phone call itself, and on incoming calls, you are paying maybe $10 for a roll of paper which will record a hundred fax messages!

In fact, as I wrote this, I was just about to replace my old fax (less than a year old!) with a new one which had a built-in answering machine, so that faxes <u>and</u> voice messages could be received on the one line.

Copiers

You can buy a new plain-paper copier for under $1000, or you may be able to find a used office-standard machine for the same sort of money. Whether or not the cost is justified will depend on the sort of work you do, but if you decide to expand into secretarial services you may well find that as with the fax, the photocopier is useful both to you (for copying client's work, etc.) and to your clients, who may be prepared to pay a little over the going rate for the convenience of having you do their copying for them.

Remember, though, that if you have a *lot* of copying to do, you may do better to go to a copy shop where the maintenance and repair of the machine are someone else's responsibility. Likewise, if you only do very little copying, a personal copier might take a long time to pay for itself. One stationer near me charges only a nickel a copy, and as I drive past the shop several times a week, I still haven't bought a photocopier.

Modem

These allow the exchange of computerized information electronically over the phone lines, and have two main uses. One is for communicating directly with your clients' computers — you can send "typed" work directly to them, over the wire, without ever actually printing it on paper — and the other is for communicating with on-line databases such as stock market quotations, airline registration systems, and so forth. This could be useful if you were heavily into personal-assistant type work.

6.5   LEGALITIES AND TECHNICALITIES

There are whole books on how to set up your own business, and they are probably worth borrowing from the library, but they often make things look more complicated than they are. Sometimes they make everything look so complicated and bureaucratic that you wonder why anyone ever even tries to run their own business: I often wonder, when I read them, how I have managed to survive while ignoring so much of their advice!

In the next few pages, we are concerned with a few **basic** legalities and technicalities that you need to know when you are setting up a home typing service.

Zoning

Unless you decide to rent an office, you will be working from home. In some areas of some cities, this may mean that you are technically breaking the law: if an area is zoned for residential use, it may be illegal to operate any kind of business.

In practice, the only time this is going to matter is if you have a constant stream of callers who are picking up and dropping off work, **and** if your neighbors object: The majority of zoning violations are reported by neighbors who are understandably annoyed about the extra traffic, difficulty of parking, strangers in the neighborhood, and so forth. They may also feel that any sort of advertising sign outside the house is inappropriate, though a small plate like a doctor's "shingle" is unlikely to offend anyone.

If you anticipate any difficulties, apply for a use permit (which is usually granted easily, without a hearing), but be aware that the best way to avoid problems with your neighbors is simply to stay on good terms with them.

Business Permits and Licenses

Because requirements for these vary enormously from city to city, never mind from state to state, the only way to find out if you need one is to ask at your local (typically city) government offices.

Such permits and licenses are rarely expensive and are easy to get: just fill in a form. If you don't have one, the penalties are rarely serious. On the other hand, if you have upset someone (we're back to the "Zoning" type of problem again), the absence of a permit can provide a stick to beat you with. All in all, it's best to get a permit if you need it.

Sales Tax

As with business permits and licenses, requirements for registration for sales tax vary widely from state to state. With a business like yours, registration may even be optional. Be *sure* you check with your own state (talking to an accountant is a good way to get information), because, while following the rules may be very easy, you can't follow what you don't know; and in this case, what you don't know COULD hurt you!

The advantage of sales tax registration is that you don't have to pay sales tax on business items — this can easily save you as much as $70 on something like a computer, and the odd cents or dollars that you save on paper and other supplies can add up surprisingly quickly.

The disadvantage of sales tax registration is that you have to give the issuing authority a lot of information which you may regard as confidential; that you have to charge sales tax to any of your clients who are not also registered; and (worst of all) that you have to add a whole new layer of bookkeeping in order to keep track of sales tax.

Taxes

Although everyone complains about the U.S. tax system, it really has only two major drawbacks. One is that taxes are ridiculously high when compared with what you get in return, and the other is that the *theoretical* powers of the IRS are frightening. Fortunately, the IRS very rarely invokes its awesome powers, and most people inside the IRS are extremely friendly and helpful: they are as fond of a quiet life as anyone else, and honest taxpayers who pay accurate taxes on time are easier to deal with. They will therefore give you a tremendous amount of help in deciding what is and is not a legitimate business expense, and in helping you to fill out the forms properly.

Having said this, you will find that filing taxes as a self-employed person requires a lot more work than filing taxes as an employee. You need to keep careful track of all your legitimate business expenses (which you can take as being any expense necessarily incurred in running the business), and at the end of the year, you need to summarize them on Schedule C.

You also need to keep track of business mileage driven in your car, because automobile expenses are prorated according to how much private mileage and how much business mileage you drive.

If you have to eat away from home, perhaps because you are visiting a distant client, you can charge only a proportion of the meal (at the time of writing, four-fifths) as a business expense. This is because the IRS makes the reasonable assumption that you have to eat anyway, so a part of the expenditure on any meal is not a business expense. I have described this example at length partly because I am fond of my food, and partly because it provides an excellent example of the intricacies of the law.

In all fairness, though, these intricacies are explained as clearly as possible in a large number of IRS publications, all of which are available free from the IRS.

Most people prefer to employ an accountant to handle their tax affairs for them, though your accountant's fees will be a lot lower if your records are well kept and up-to-date, preferably with the type of spreadsheet program in Chapter 3, instead of being in shoe-boxes. If you use an accountant, be sure that it is someone who is personally recommended to you, or use an established tax preparation service like H & R Block. You may even find that if you are prepared to hack your way through all the IRS literature, you can do your tax preparation yourself, and have the advantage of knowing what you are doing instead of trusting someone else.

Self-Employment Tax — Something that most employees know nothing about is the separate self-employment tax, quite separate from federal income tax, that is imposed on self-employed people. This takes the place of FICA contributions for an employee (which are split between the employer and the employee), and comes as a nasty shock when you first learn about it.

After you have computed your gross taxable income (in other words, before taking allowances for yourself, your spouse, etc.) the self-employment tax is calculated straight off the top of this. In other words, using 1990 figures, if your gross income was $15,000 and your expenses were $5000, your gross taxable income would be $10,000.

For federal income tax, you might take $2000 each for yourself and your spouse, and a $5000 standard deduction, totalling $9000. This would leave you with $1000 of taxable income, you might think.

Well, it would; but you would also need to fill in Schedule SE, and pay the self employment tax on the whole $10,000. Nor is this a small tax: it was just over 13 per cent at the time of writing, so they would hit you for over $1300.

State Income Taxes — These are increasingly figured on the same basis as the federal tax, but you must still remember to file — and, of course, to pay!

Insurance

Basically, it is a good idea to have three kinds of insurance: a good broker can help you with all three.

One is obviously health insurance, and you have to remember that you will no longer have an employer to take care of this for you.

The second is insurance for the tools of your trade. Here, you can insure just against theft (worth considering if you have an expensive computer set-up!), and against failure. The second type of insurance is often called a "maintenance contract," but it's still insurance; you may do best here by asking about extended guarantees when you buy your equipment.

The third type of insurance covers against "long shots" such as a client tripping over a rug in your house, breaking a leg, and suing you for thousands. Such "liability" insurance is normally very cheap indeed.

6.6   COPING WITH TOO MUCH WORK

The easiest way to do this is to start saying "no," but the mere fact that you have more work than you can handle is a good sign that you could charge more.

Charging More

Exactly **how much** more you charge is up to you, but a rise of less than $1 per hour is hardly worth making, and more than about $2.50 an hour may well start losing clients.

You may also start charging new clients more, but leave established clients at the old rate; or (for example) put up the rate for old clients by $1 and for new clients by $2.

You may lose a few customers, and even suffer a (very slight) drop in income for a few weeks — but if you really do have more work than you can handle, you'll soon make up the work, and you'll be charging more for it!

Work-sharing

Another possibility is to find someone else who offers the same sort of service that you do, and passing on extra work. In return, they pass extra work on to you, when you are going through a lean patch. In fact, this isn't a bad idea when you're getting started!

Employing People

There is no doubt that some people have built whole businesses on the kind of service I have described in this book, and even become millionaires. While I wouldn't dream of discouraging you from this, I would say that it is a tremendous amount of work and responsibility — and that quite honestly, it goes beyond the scope of this book, which is about how you can earn money at home. If you are doing so well that you can consider expanding in this way, there are plenty of other books which tell you how to do it. And may I be the first to wish you the very best of luck!

7.0 RESOURCES

You are not alone. This book is here to help you, and so are many other books, government and other institutions, and people who work in many capacities. The government's Small Business Administration is one such agency (see page 128). They have all kinds of literature which they will send you in response to your letter or a phone call.

The "front line" of assistance, though, comes from three local sources: your local Yellow Pages, your local Chamber of Commerce, and your local library.

7.1 HOW TO READ THE YELLOW PAGES

Telling you how to read the Yellow Pages may sound silly, but in truth, you may not have realized how useful they can be. You can do a lot worse than to browse through your local Yellow Pages, not looking at the individual companies, but at the *types* of companies listed. Although these headings are summarized in several pages at the front, you get more of a *feel* for the businesses by flicking through the book, and seeing how big the advertisements are, and what they say about the companies.

For example, opening my Yellow Pages at random, I see the following headings **on one page:**

CATERING EQUIPMENT
CATERING SUPPLIES — FOOD AND DRINK
CATTLE BREEDERS AND DEALERS
CEILING CONTRACTORS
CEILINGS — SUSPENDED
CELLULAR RADIO

This gives me a couple of ideas. For example, CATERING SUPPLIES — FOOD AND DRINK might well need price-lists or even menus typed up pretty regularly. Also, I had no idea there were so many businesses specializing in suspended ceilings. Maybe they need proposals typed up; from the number of them listed and the size of their advertisements, it looks like pretty big business.

On the other hand, CATTLE BREEDERS AND DEALERS has only a couple of entries, and they are in small type with no display ads. I imagine that cattle dealing takes place at markets or auctions, or on the premises of the dealer himself. If a farmer wants a new bull, he's going to look at the animal himself, so there's unlikely to be much call for typing here. Also, those farms may be way out in the country — it wouldn't be economical to work for them anyway.

You can see from this that the Yellow Pages tell you far more than the name of a plumber when you want one: they provide a picture of the businesses in *your* community.

7.2   CHAMBERS OF COMMERCE

In France, the term for **Chamber of Commerce** translates roughly as **Initiative Syndicate**. This is much more descriptive than the American term. A Chamber of Commerce is (or should be) a syndicate of business people who take the initiative in promoting their own companies *and their communities*. They believe that what's good for their town is good for them, and that what's good for them is good for their town.

In all fairness, some Chambers of Commerce are a lot livelier than others. At their worst, they are little more than a social club for the local business people to meet one another for a drink every now and then. At their best, they are wonderful storehouses of information and a tremendous source of contacts for *your* business.

Nor can you judge a Chamber of Commerce by its offices. Often, the office itself is an obscure little room somewhere. If you want to get through to them, you can either join or just write to them. Normally, just writing is quite enough: these people really *want* to encourage local business, and if they see you as a potential asset, they'll help you.

As usual, a preliminary phone call will get the basic information from the receptionist: who to write to, what sort of literature the Chamber of Commerce produces, and so forth — and then a letter to the contact person will get you a friendly letter back. Where it goes from there is up to you. It is also worth knowing that many Chambers of Commerce administer programs whereby retired business people will give advice — often free or sometimes at nominal cost — on any business problems you may have. One such program, which your Chamber of Commerce should know about, is SCORE, the Service Corps of Retired Executives.

In fact, the deeper you get into the workings of the Chamber of Commerce, the more you are likely to find what they do, and it is all likely to help you. The only problem is that it often takes a while to find out how the Chamber works; because it is primarily a network of local contacts, you have to get into that network. After a while, you may well decide to join: it can be an excellent investment, and it isn't *that* expensive. As already mentioned, joining in your first year can be an excellent way of getting your name known around town, and you can reassess at the end of the year whether it was worth joining.

7.3   YOUR LOCAL LIBRARY — A MAJOR RESOURCE

The reference librarian at your local library can turn out to be one of your best friends. She (or sometimes he) is a tremendous repository of information, and no one else is likely to have a better idea of where to look in order to find something out. Although some librarians may *look* rather forbidding, the vast majority of them really enjoy a challenge; it's the easy questions, the ones that anyone could answer for themselves if they bothered to look on the shelves, that they regard as a waste of time.

From your point of view, the best thing they can do is to guide you around the maze of assorted business directories that *you* can use to increase *your* business.

Business Directories and How to Use Them

Normally, there will be two separate stocks of the kind of trade directories that you need. The big national ones, which you are likely to find less useful (but see below) are normally on the open shelves, while the local ones are by the librarian's desk.

Their position reflects their usefulness: the books that librarians keep by their desks are the ones that the librarians themselves consult often, and which they also have to watch in case they go "walkies" in the hands of people who are more enthusiastic than honest.

National Directories

These normally occupy several **feet** of shelving and provide an excellent cross-section of the nation's business. Their only drawback is that you are not likely to get much business from the mega-corporations that appear in the national directories; it is hard to imagine Donald Trump running across the street to get his typing done!

They are useful, though, for other purposes. For example, one directory lists every trade name in use in the United States, and who owns it. Another tells you how much different companies spend on advertising, while a third lists the number of employees and the revenue (in dollars per year) of literally thousands of companies nationwide. While you are unlikely to deal with these big corporations yourself, your *clients* may well deal with them, and five minutes spent checking the information on a client's own customers can make you look very clever indeed.

You can also use these directories to create mailing lists. Although the people to whom you sell the lists *could* use the directories themselves, the chances are that they do not have the time to do so. There are dozens — perhaps hundreds — of these directories, which are often updated every year: the list below is intended merely to give a sampling of what is available. The ultimate directory must be *The Directory of Directories*, which simply lists all the other directories that are available.

Barron's — Major colleges and other institutions of higher learning.

Directory of Associations — Voluntary organizations as well as businesses, clubs, and many others are covered in this massive multi-part book.

Foundation Grants Index — Lists bodies who make academic and other grants — invaluable for an academic mailing list!

Literary Market Place — Usually just known as **LMP**, this normally lives by the librarian's counter: it is *the* guide to the publishing world.

Lovejoy's — Covers similar ground to *Barron's*, above.

Martindale-Hubbard Directory — All major law firms, broken down into areas.

Standard and Poor's Directory of American Businesses — All major corporations in the US, with financial and other management data.

State Directories

The worth of these will depend on the state you live in. In California, for example, a state directory is almost as awe-inspiring as a national one: multi-million dollar companies follow one another across the pages, column upon column. In smaller or less heavily populated states, though, a good state directory can be as useful as a local one — and, of course, if you live in Rhode Island, the two are likely to be the same directory! The uses of local directories are discussed below.

Local Directories

This is where the real meat lies: this is where you can find the companies in *your* community who will hire *you*.

Chamber of Commerce Directories — these tend to contain nothing more than Yellow Pages-type listings, but they do have one big advantage over the Yellow Pages. Most Chambers of Commerce tend to stick together, and if you work for one member of a Chamber of Commerce it can lead to work with another member, too. This may be by personal recommendation (they call you) or it may just give you the selling edge to be able to say, "Well, I have already worked for Joe Smith at the Santa Maria Widget Corporation. Why don't you call him and check me out?"

City Directories — The two best-known publishers of city directories are Haines (with the Criss-Cross directories) and Polk's.

You may learn more about your home city than you ever thought possible with these directories: weather statistics, median home values, major industries, sports and much else. They typically have listings rather like the Yellow Pages, and then a whole lot more besides. They even tell you who lives in which house on each street: The sheer amount of information they contain is a little disturbing. As one librarian put it, "Big Brother is watching you — and making a profit out of it, too!"

Clubs and Organizations — a much less overwhelming sort of directory, also held behind the desk in most libraries, will contain the names, addresses, and contact numbers of many volunteer organizations, clubs, associations, and so forth, many of whom may require typing done from time to time. Samples taken at random from one in my local library include Self-Help Hard of Hearing; several local gun clubs; the Los Padres Artists' Guild; and many more. Any or all of these organizations might need occasional typing, and most of them even give you the name of the contact person. The chances are that a person who is involved in one thing is involved in several, so while an inquiry letter (page 86) may produce no work from the organization you thought you were contacting, it may well produce work from elsewhere!

County Directories — These are, again, in a sort of Yellow Pages format, but they contain a good deal more local information, and the individual listings are generally more informative. In addition to the name, address and phone number of the company, there will usually be a brief summary of the sort of work the company does (great for checking whether your specialized knowledge meets their needs!) and other information including the name of the owner or other key personnel, the number of employees, how long the company has been in business, and whether the business is a sole proprietorship, a partnership or a corporation.

Economic Development Brochures — Most cities have economic development boards or councils, whose job it is to lure businesses into their city. The great advantage of these brochures is that they tell you something about the various businesses in an area — size, assets, number of employees, and so forth — rather than just giving bald listings.

Job Banks – Some cities or areas will have directories of the area's principal employers. Not only do these directories list companies and what they do, they also have a comprehensive section on exactly what different types of companies there are. Did you know exactly how geophysicists earn a living, other than in universities? I had a vague idea, but I learned a lot more by reading the back of the Southern California Job Bank (part of the Job Bank series of books).

7.4   MAGAZINES AND PUBLICATIONS

There are numerous books and magazines available these days designed to assist the small business owner. Some are wonderful; some are not so wonderful. Just about any magazine will allow you to see a sample issue prior to subscribing, so take a look before you commit. If you can find the magazine on your newsstand, this is the best method. Sometimes, however, you will receive literature through the mail telling you about how wonderful some new publication is ... it may be, but *check it out*!

There are some newsletters and magazines we would like to recommend to you that we have found quite useful and that seem to have information that is accurate and timely. While this is not a complete list by any means, it will give you some places to look:

Barbara Brabec's National Home Business Report
This publication comes out quarterly and is "dedicated to helping small businesses grow." You can find out about subscribing by sending a letter to:

The National Home Business Report
P.O. Box 2137
Naperville, IL 60567

You can obtain a sample issue for $5.00.

Women & Co.
"Strategies, Ideas, Solutions for the Business Owner"
This is a monthly newsletter published by Women & Company, which is a division of Bantam Doubleday Dell Publishing Group, Inc. A one-year subscription is $49.00. If you are interested in subscribing contact:

Women & Co.
P.O. Box 10769
Des Moines, IA 50340

The National Association for the Cottage Industry
P.O. Box 14850
Chicago, IL 60614
(312) 472-8116

Annual membership in this association costs $45.00 and includes an annual subscription to *COTTAGE CONNECTION*. They also provide information, networking and the following benefits: access to professional guidance, car rental discounts, discounts on group health & life insurance, discount on dental and optical insurance, disability insurance, discounts on subscriptions to business magazines.

Entrepreneur
Subscription Department
2392 Morse Avenue
P.O. Box 19787
Irvine, CA 92713-9441
(800) 421-2300 Outside of California
(800) 352-7449 in California

ENTREPRENEUR is a monthly publication designed to inform, educate and assist the individual who has dreams and goals above and beyond those of working for someone else. Each issue comes packed with ideas and inspiration that will help you stay in touch with what other people are doing to be successful.

Nation's Business
P.O. Box 51062
Boulder, CO 80321-1062
(800) 638-6582
(800) 352-1450 in MD

This is a monthly publication that covers just about every aspect of the business world, with considerable attention being given to women in business, entrepreneurs and small businesses.

In Business
Box 323
Emmaus, PA 18049
(215) 967-4135

This is another publication designed to help the small business owner. Worth taking a look at!

7.5   SMALL BUSINESS ADMINISTRATION

You may call or write to the SBA office nearest you to ask about their programs which can help you get started in your typing business. Look over the addresses on the following pages for your nearest office.

REGION I

Areas Served: Connecticut, Maine, Massachusetts, New Hampshire, Rhode Island, Vermont

Regional Office:
Small Business Administration
155 Federal Street, 9th Floor
Boston, MA 02110
(617) 451-2023

District Offices:

10 Causeway Street, Room 265
Boston, MA 02222-1093
(617) 565-5590

Federal Building
40 Western Ave., Room 512
Augusta, ME 04330
(207) 622-8378

55 Pleasant Street, Room 210
Concord, NH 03302-1257
(603) 225-1400

Federal Building
330 Main Street, 2nd Floor
Hartford, CT 06106
(203) 240-4700

Federal Building
87 State Street, Room 205
Montpelier, VT 05602
(802) 828-4474

380 Westminster Mall, 5th Floor
Providence, RI 02903
(401) 528-4561

1550 Main Street, Room 212
Springfield, MA 01103
(413) 785-0268

REGION II

Areas Served: New Jersey, New York, Puerto Rico, Virgin Islands

Regional Office:
Small Business Administration
26 Federal Plaza, Room 31-08
New York, NY 10278
(212) 264-7772

District Offices:

Carlos Chardon Avenue, Rm 691
Hato Rey, PR 00915
(809) 766-4002

60 Park Place, 4th Floor
Newark, NJ 07102
(201) 645-2434

26 Federal Plaza, Room 3100
New York, NY 10278
(212) 264-4355

100 S. Clinton St., Rm 1071
Syracuse, NY 13260
(315) 423-5383

111 W. Huron Street, Room 1311
Buffalo, NY 14202
(716) 846-4301

333 E. Water Street, 4th Floor
Elmira, NY 14901
(607) 734-8130

100 State Street, Room 601
Rochester, NY 14614
(716) 263-6700

445 Broadway, Room 222
Albany, NY 12207
(518) 431-4261

2600 Mt. Ephrain Ave.
Camden, NJ 08104
(609) 757-5183

4C & 4D Este Sion Frm., Room 7
St. Croix, VI 00820
(809) 778-5380

Veterans Drive, Room 283
St. Thomas, VI 00801
(809) 774-8530

REGION III

Areas Served: Delaware, District of
Columbia, Maryland, Pennsylvania,
Virginia, West Virginia

Regional Office:
Small Business Administration
475 Allendale Road, Suite 201
King of Prussia, PA 19406
(215) 962-3700

District Offices:

10 N. Calvert Street, 3rd Floor
Baltimore, MD 21202
(410) 962-4392

168 W. Main Street, 5th Floor
Clarkesburg, WV 26301
(304) 623-5631

475 Allendale Road, Suite 201
King of Prussia, PA 19406
(215) 962-3846

960 Penn Avenue, 5th Floor
Pittsburgh, PA 15222
(412) 644-2780

400 N. 8th Street, Room 3015
Richmond, VA 23240
(804) 771-2617

1111 18th Street, 6th Floor
Washington, DC 20036
(202) 634-1500

550 Eagan Street, Room 309
Charleston, WV 25301
(304) 347-5220

100 Chestnut Street, Room 309
Harrisburg, PA 17101
(717) 782-3840

20 N. Pennsylvania Ave.
Room 2327
Wilkes-Barre, PA 18702
(717) 826-6497

920 N. King Street, Suite 412
Wilmington, DE 19801
(302) 573-6295

REGION IV

Areas Served: Alabama, Florida,
Georgia, Kentucky, Mississippi, North
Carolina, South Carolina, Tennessee

Regional Office:
Small Business Administration
1375 Peachtree St, NE, 5th Floor
Atlanta, GA 30367-8102
(404) 347-2797

District Offices:

1720 Peachtree Rd., NW, 6th Floor
Atlanta, GA 30309
(404) 347-4749

2121 8th Ave., N., Suite 200
Birmingham, AL 35203-2398
(205) 731-1344

1835 Assembly Street, Room 358
Columbia, SC 29202
(803) 765-5376

1320 S. Dixie Highway, Suite 501
Coral Gables, FL 33146
(305) 536-5521

100 W. Capitol Street, Suite 400
Jackson, MS 39201
(601) 965-4378

7825 Haymeadows Way
Suite 100-B
Jacksonville, FL 32256-7504
(904) 443-1900

600 Dr. M.L.K. Jr. Pl., Room 188
Louisville, KY 40202
(502) 582-5978

One Hancock Plaza, Suite 1001
Gulfport, MS 39501-7758
(601) 863-4449

501 East Polk Street, Suite 104
Tampa, FL 33602-3945
(813)228-2594

REGION V

Areas Served: Illinois, Indiana,
Michigan, Minnesota, Ohio, Wisconsin

Regional Office:
Small Business Administration
Federal Building
230 S. Dearborn Street, Rm 510
Chicago, IL 60604-1593
(312) 353-0359

District Offices:

219 South Dearborn St., Rm 437
Chicago, IL 60604-1779
(312) 353-4528

1240 E. 9th Street, Room 317
Cleveland, OH 44199
(216) 522-4180

85 Marconi Boulevard
Columbus, OH 43215
(614) 469-6860

477 Michigan Avenue, Room 515
Detroit, MI 48226
(313) 226-6075

429 N. Pennsylvania St.,
Suite 100
Indianapolis, IN 46204-1873
(317) 226-7272

212 E. Washington Ave., Rm 213
Madison, WI 53703
(608) 264-5261

100 N. 6th St., Suite 610
Minneapolis, MN 55403-1563
(612) 370-2324

550 Main Street, Room 5028
Cincinnati, OH 45202
(513) 684-2814

300 S. Front Street
Marquette, MI 49885
(906) 225-1108

310 W. Wisconsin Ave., Suite 400
Milwaukee, WI 53203
(414) 297-3941

511 W. Capitol Street, Suite 302
Springfield, IL 62704
(217) 492-4416

500 S. Barstow Commo, Room 17
Eau Claire, WI 54701
(715) 834-1573

REGION VI

Areas Served: Arkansas, Louisiana,
New Mexico, Oklahoma, Texas

Regional Office:
Small Business Administration
8625 King George Dr., Bldg. C
Dallas, TX 75235-3391
(214) 767-7643

District Offices:

625 Silver Ave., SW, Suite 320
Albuquerque, NM 87102
(505) 766-1870

10737 Gateway W., Suite 320
El Paso, TX 79935
(915) 540-5586

222 East Van Buren St., Rm 500
(Lower Rio Grande Valley)
Harlingen, TX 78550
(512) 427-8533

9301 SW Freeway, Suite 550
Houston, TX 77074
(713) 773-6500

320 W. Capitol Ave., Room 601
Little Rock, AR 72201
(501) 324-5871

1611 Tenth Street, Suite 200
Lubbock, TX 79401
(806) 743-7462

1661 Canal Street, Suite 2000
New Orleans, LA 70112
(504) 589-6685

200 N. W. 5th Street, Suite 670
Oklahoma City, OK 73102
(405) 231-4301

7400 Blanco Road, Suite 200
San Antonio, TX 78216
(512) 229-4535

400 Mann Street, Suite 403
Corpus Christi, TX 78401
(512) 888-3331

819 Taylor Street, Room 8A-27
Ft. Worth, TX 76102
(817) 334-3777

300 E. 8th Street, Room 520
Austin, TX 78701
(512) 482-5288

505 E. Travis
Marshall, TX 75670
(903) 935-5257

500 Fannin Street, Room 8A-08
Shreveport, LA 71101
(318) 226-5196

REGION VII

Areas Served: Iowa, Kansas, Missouri, Nebraska

Regional Office:
911 Walnut Street, 13th Floor
Kansas City, MO 64106
(816) 426-3608

District Offices:

373 Collins Road NE, Room 100
Cedar Rapids, IA 52402-3118
(319) 393-8630

210 Walnut Street, Room 749
Des Moines, IA 50309
(515) 284-4762

323 W. 8th Street, Suite 501
Kansas City, MO 64105
(816) 374-6762

11145 Mill Valley Road
Omaha, NB 68154
(402) 221-3604

815 Olive Street, Room 242
St. Louis, MO 63101
(314) 539-6600

110 E. Waterman Street
Wichita, KS 67202
(316) 269-6273

620 S. Glenstone St., Suite 110
Springfield, MO 65802-3200
(417) 864-7670

REGION VIII

Areas Served: Colorado, Montana, North Dakota, South Dakota, Utah, Wyoming

Regional Office:
Small Business Administration
999 18th Street, Suite 701
Denver, CO 80202
(303) 294-7186

District Offices:

Federal Building
100 East B Street, Room 4001
Casper, WY 82602-2839
(307) 261-5761

721 19th Street, Room 407
Denver, CO 80201-0660
(303) 294-7186

657 2nd Ave. N., Room 218
Fargo, ND 58108-3086
(701) 239-5131

301 S. Park
Helena, MT 59626
(406)449-5381

125 S. State Street, Room 2237
Salt Lake City, UT 84138-1195
(801) 524-5800

101 S. Main Ave., Suite 101
Sioux Falls, SD 57102-0527
(605) 330-4231

REGION IX

Areas Served: Arizona, California,
Hawaii, Nevada, Pacific Islands

Regional Office:
Small Buisness Administration
Federal Building
71 Stevenson Street, 20th Floor
San Francisco, CA 94105-2939
(415) 744-6409

District Offices:

2719 N. Air Fresno Dr.
Fresno, CA 93727-1547
(805) 487-5189

330 N. Grand Blvd., Suite 1200
Glendale, CA 91203-2304
(818) 552-3210

300 Ala Moana, Room 2213
Honolulu, HI 96850-4981
(808) 541-2990

301 E. Stewart St., Room 301
Las Vegas, NV 89125-2527
(702) 388-6611

2005 N. Central Ave., 5th Floor
Phoenix, AZ 85004
(602) 640-2316

880 Front Street, Suite 4-S-29
San Diego, CA 92188-0270
(619) 557-5440

901 W. Civic Ctr. Dr., Suite 160
Santa Ana, CA 92703-2352
(714) 836-2494

Pacific Daily News Bdg, Room 508
Agana, GM 96910
(671) 472-7277

660 J Street, Room 215
Sacramento, CA 95814-2413
(916) 498-6660

50 S. Virginia St., Room 238
Reno, NV 89505-3216
(702) 784-5268

6477 Telephone Rd., Suite 10
Ventura, CA 93003-4459
(805) 642-1866

REGION X

Areas Served: Alaska, Idaho, Oregon,
Washington

Regional Office:
Small Business Administration
2615 4th Avenue, Room 440
(206) 553-1455

134

District Offices:

222 W. 8th Ave., Room A36
Anchorage, AK 99513
(907) 271-4022

1020 Main Street, Suite 290
Boise, ID 83702
(208) 334-1696

222 S. W. Columbia, Suite 500
Portland, OR 97201-6605
(503) 326-2682

915 Second Ave., Room 1792
Seattle, WA 98174-1088
(206) 553-5534

W. 601 1st Avenue, 10th Floor E.
Spokane, WA 99204
(509) 353-2800

7.6   FOR WOMEN ONLY

There are several organizations which exist *solely* to help women in business. For example, the Small Business Administration operates the <u>Women's Network for Entrepreneurial Training</u> (WNET); your local office can give you details of this, and the <u>Office of Women's Business Ownership</u>. You may also want to contact the following:

National Association of Women Business Owners (NAWBO)
1413 "K" Street NW, Suite 637
Washington, DC 20005
Telephone (301) 608-2590

This is a modestly-sized organization which lobbies the government on behalf of women who are starting their own businesses; they also have a Leadership Institute, which is designed to help women develop management skills.

The National Federation of Business and Professional Women's Clubs, Inc.
2012 Massachusetts Avenue NW
Washington, DC 20036
Telephone (202) 293-1100

This is exactly what its name suggests: there are over 3,500 chapters and over 120,000 members.

American Women's Economic Development Corporation (AWED)
71 Vanderbilt Avenue #320
New York, NY 10020
Telephone (212) 692-9100

This organization offers programs on starting and running small businesses. Counseling is available for a small fee at the following telephone numbers:

New York City, Alaska, Hawaii: (212) 692-9100
New York State: (800) 442-AWED
Elsewhere: (800) 222-AWED

National Association of Secretarial Services (NASS)
3637 Fourth Street North, Suite 330
St. Petersburg, FL 33704
Telephone (800) 237-1462

While this isn't actually just a women's organization, it's common knowledge that most secretarial service owner/operators are women. this wonderful organization is not only nationwide, but worldwide, and their goal is to keep secretarial service owners (including those working from their homes) in contact with one another and to share secrets, problems, solutions, etc. Conferences are held each year in different parts of the country to review new technology, the best ways of doing things and how best to help clients while keeping the business owner's interests right up front as well.

7.7   CHECKLIST FOR YOUR OFFICE SUPPLIES

Use this list to help you get started with respect to the supplies you may need on hand to properly and efficiently perform your typing services. You may need other supplies not listed, or some of those shown here may not be necessary for you.

CONSUMABLES

Paper Group:

- [ ] Headed paper (letterhead)
- [ ] Business cards
- [ ] Continuation paper
- [ ] Fanfold (computer/continuous feed) paper (if you use a dot matrix printer)
- [ ] Labels
- [ ] Envelopes (large)
- [ ] Envelopes (small)
- [ ] Index cards
- [ ] Client file sheets (page 141)
- [ ] Staples
- [ ] Paper clips

Writing Group:

- [ ] Pencils/leads
- [ ] Erasers
- [ ] Pens/refills
- [ ] "Highlighter" markers
- [ ] Ribbons
- [ ] Floppy disks
- [ ] Correction fluid

Filing Group

- ❑ Hanging files
- ❑ File folders
- ❑ File tabs or labels

Miscellaneous

- ❑ Postage stamps
- ❑ Express Delivery envelopes
- ❑ Rubber bands
- ❑ Adhesive tape
- ❑ Calendar

NON-CONSUMABLES

- ❑ In/Out/Pending trays
- ❑ Filing cabinets
- ❑ Looseleaf binders
- ❑ Floppy disk storage boxes
- ❑ Calculator
- ❑ Ruler
- ❑ Scissors
- ❑ Stapler
- ❑ Staple remover
- ❑ Waste basket
- ❑ Letter opener

7.8   SETTING UP A CLIENT FILE

Photocopy page 141 and use it as a basis for your client file. You will need one sheet for each client. Fill it in as follows:

Client Name — use the name that the client uses for his business, *in full, EXACTLY* as it appears on the company letterhead. In other words, if it is The Widget Corporation of Iowa, Inc., write that, not just "Widget Corp."   I used to be a director of a company called TriStar Communications, and you wouldn't *believe* how many "TriStars" and "Tri-Stars" there are in the world.

Address — Street name, apartment or suite number on the first line; city, state and zip code on the next line.

Contact Name — Write down the name of the person you normally deal with, and his or her job title, and any odd pronunciations. For example, you might write: Herbert "Herb" Liwitov (Liv-it-off), Assistant Sales Manager.

Phone Number — With the area code, even if it's local. Write down the extension for your contact, and don't forget a fax number if it's appropriate.

Date First Contacted is self-explanatory, but **Follow-up** will remind you to follow up your initial contacts.

Notes can be used for all sorts of things. They are to help you give a personal service, and (in some cases) to remember who the client is and what he or she looks like. You might write something like: "Short, dark-haired, balding. Likes baseball (Dodgers). Wife (Alison) works for Smith & Son. Two small children: Steve (born 3/3/88) and Anne (2/7/90). Sometimes a slow payer, but always pays eventually."

Obviously, you never let *anyone* see this file!

Job Log — The "Date" entry is obvious, and the "Description" is to jog your memory: it might read "3-page letter" or "127-page manuscript" or "6 pages of sales figures." The "Fee" entry is to remind you what he paid last time for comparable work, and to help you work out what to charge next time, as well as for your bookkeeping records. Put a tick alongside the fee (with the date, if you like) when you are actually paid. For split fees, use a cross: one stroke for the first half or deposit, the cross-stroke for the second half or remainder.

The additional blank space at the foot of the sheet can be used for more notes. If your contact name (or anything else) changes, make up a new client sheet rather than crossing things out and trying to write in the new information.

CLIENT FILE SHEET

CLIENT NAME_____

ADDRESS_____

CITY/STATE/ZIP CODE_____

Contact Name_____

Phone No. (   )_____ Extension_____ Fax (   )_____

Date first contacted_____ Follow-up_____

Notes_____

_____

_____

JOB LOG

Date	**Description**	**Fee**
_____	_____	$_____
_____	_____	$_____
_____	_____	$_____
_____	_____	$_____
_____	_____	$_____
_____	_____	$_____
_____	_____	$_____
_____	_____	$_____
_____	_____	$_____
_____	_____	$_____
_____	_____	$_____
_____	_____	$_____
_____	_____	$_____

7.9 STATE ABBREVIATIONS

Quick — what's the state abbreviation for Arkansas, Arizona, Alaska, Alabama? If you have to guess (especially if you're tired), you could make a mistake; and if that important client letter that you were supposed to send to Arizona (AZ) gets addressed to Arkansas (AR), it can take the Postal Service two weeks to get it back to you for correction of the address! It's very simple (and smart!) to keep a listing handy on your desk or wall where you can see it at a glance; photocopy this page and put it somewhere convenient so you'll always have the right information.

Alabama	AL	Montana	MT
Alaska	AK	Nebraska	NE
Arizona	AZ	Nevada	NV
Arkansas	AR	New Hampshire	NH
California	CA	New Jersey	NJ
Colorado	CO	New Mexico	NM
Connecticut	CT	New York	NY
Delaware	DE	North Carolina	NC
D.C.	DC	North Dakota	ND
Florida	FL	Ohio	OH
Georgia	GA	Oklahoma	OK
Hawaii	HI	Oregon	OR
Idaho	ID	Pennsylvania	PA
Illinois	IL	Rhode Island	RI
Indiana	IN	South Carolina	SC
Iowa	IA	South Dakota	SD
Kansas	KS	Tennessee	TN
Kentucky	KY	Texas	TX
Louisiana	LA	Utah	UT
Maine	ME	Vermont	VT
Maryland	MD	Virginia	VA
Massachusetts	MA	Washington	WA
Michigan	MI	West Virginia	WV
Minnesota	MN	Wisconsin	WI
Mississippi	MS	Wyoming	WY
Missouri	MO		

NOTES

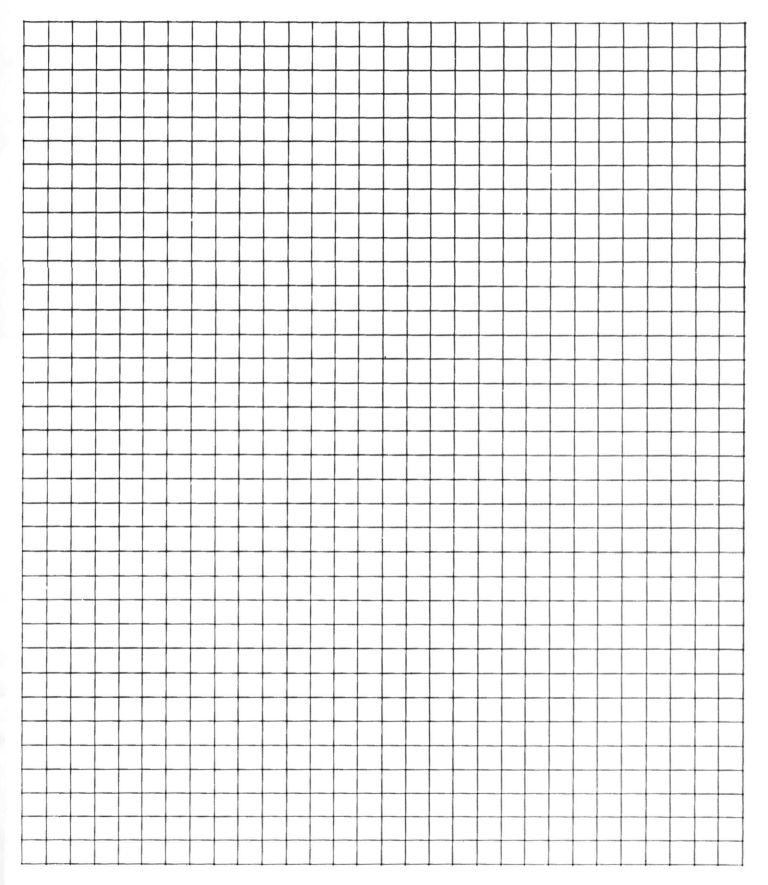

NOTES

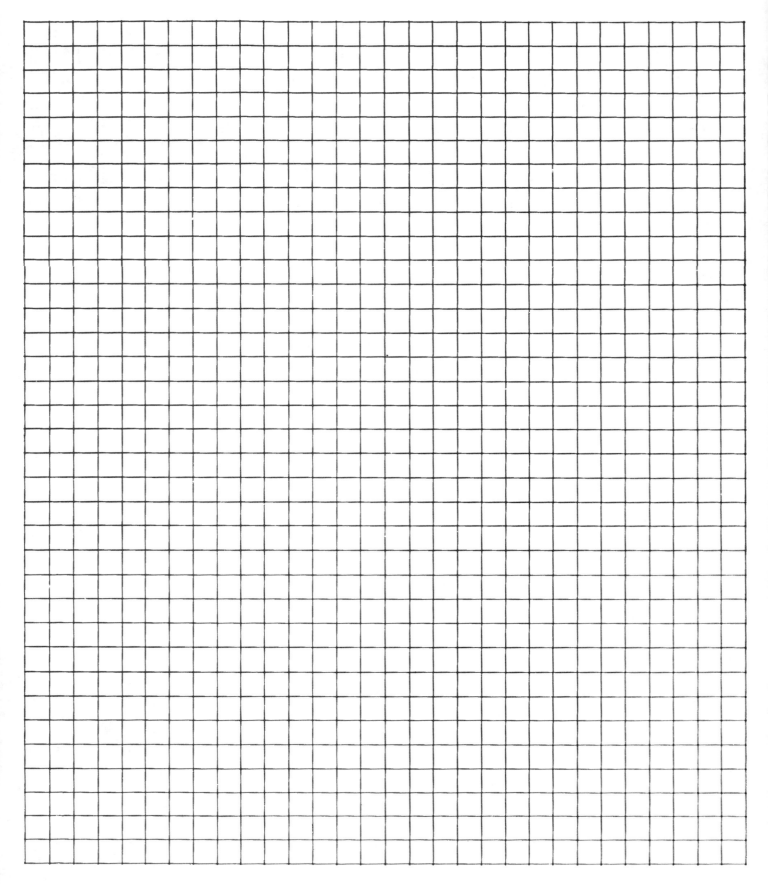

NOTES

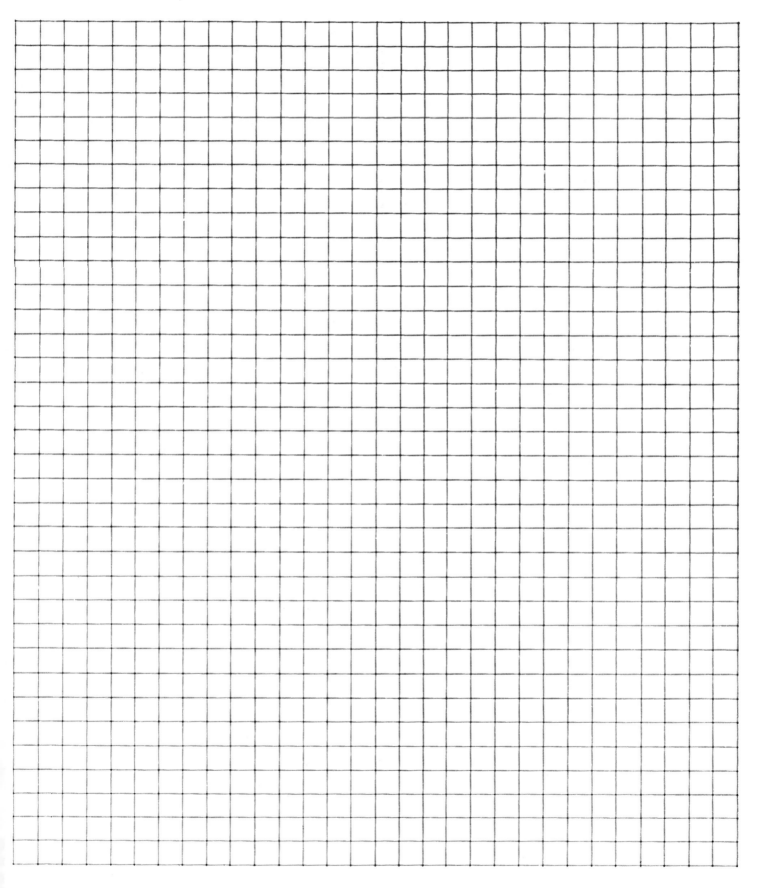

NOTES

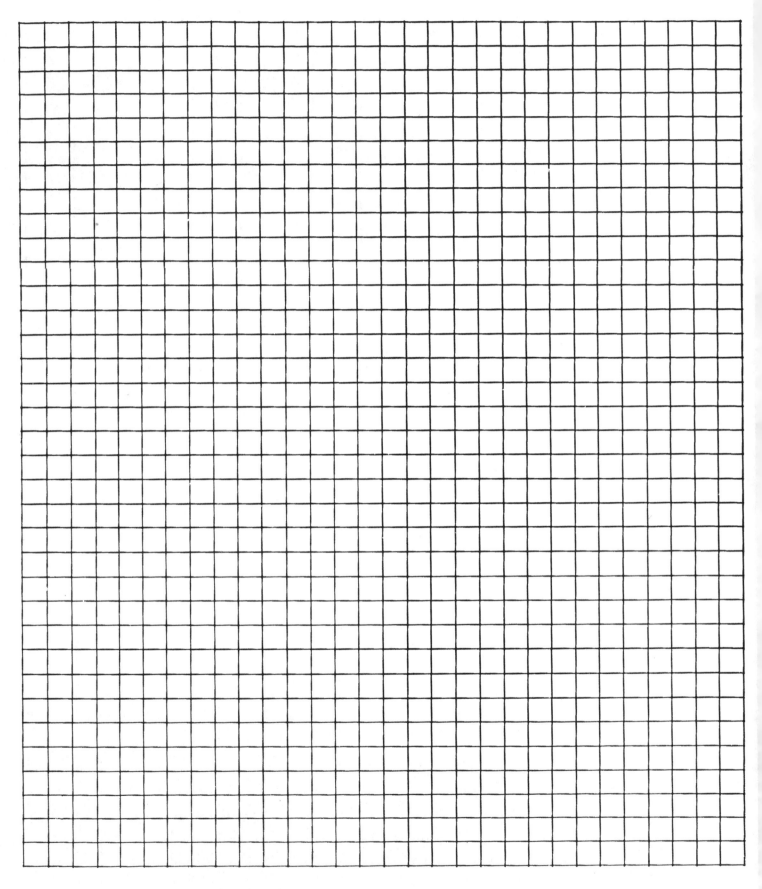